THE ART OF
CHRISTIANITY

THE ART OF CHRISTIANITY

JeJa ReRa

To order additional copies of this book, contact:
Xlibris Corporation
1-888-795-4274
www.Xlibris.com
Orders@Xlibris.com
32688

DEDICATION

For a dream known as Jeja, don't spell Jesus Y-a-h-e-a-w.

For Susan, a friend of the family whom I saw in a Christian Science church when I was just a little boy. There should be a house of safety somewhere in the world where art is kept sacred.

For Mary Baker Eddy, a woman who had the nerve to try to understand science, and in whose footprints I should walk again.

ACKNOWLEDGMENTS

I would like to thank a priest who saved my life, my soul and many others'. Their families, I imagine, helped them appear in my life. For my mother who has written books about Christian manuscripts throughout her whole life, my father, who left his father's land and the Presbyterian Church to look for heavy particle collisions in atomic physics, my brother who also acted like the backbone I needed, and my sister whom I need as much forgiveness from as she deserves.

This book could not have been done without *soul*; *love*; woman; mankind; everyone who has lived right down to the first algae cells of life into religion, division, and the NAACP; the American people; the presidents of the United States; William C. Ackerley, an African American who raped me emotionally as well as physically; my own attempt to escape the human capacity to hate; the colleges I have attended; my agent, Andrew Hamilton; of course, the inspiration for all my work, Martin Luther King Sr. and his son, Martin Luther King Jr.; and lastly, the cats and dogs of the world today, who will help us protect ourselves for a very long time.

INTRODUCTION

Most artists these days are in a bit of dilemma. This author included, there is a serious lack of originality. It seems impossible to create in the world with an intention of any true merit. The 9-11 disaster, the consequences of the invasion of American thought by subversive thinking deserve a brief note on art. The sense of undermining world security through thought and religion is turning out to destabilize almost everything. The Chinese seem not to be afraid of anything at all, Africa is still experiencing birth pains, South America needs help as well. The global community should learn quickly how to organize a safe environment.

The progression of events is misleading in a number of serious ways. One of these is in the capacity of individuals to restrain themselves. Most people in the West feel that they are losing control. Most groups of people in the United States are being split by the forces of ordinary individuals who may not be able to answer plainly to the law. All there is to say about how free this country has become is that during the 9-11 disaster, none of us saw the terrorism coming, and little mention needs to be made that the events may not happen twice.

From the self-reflective position, this book too is a moral crime. The language is Western, and if I had had my way, I can write it in Gaelic; ancient Chinese; or, most authoritatively in this country; the original language of the Native Americans. There is an interesting oral history in my family. As a Scot, long ago, it is said that travelers came across the ocean from England tens of thousands of years ago to "America." Prehistory is one thing, while the present state of invasion of the two Western continents is another. So the reader will have to excuse my employment of typically Christian language. In a way, and small-community language is the kind I speak, and I must say, here and now, that I do not completely believe that one can communicate with more than a handful of people. That is one of the problems with writing's difference with speech.

Similarly, one should definitely think carefully about a thought style. I have written many books, one of which explains something about the internal life shape of the person. We are usually one way or the other, but in reality, no such fixation is possible. I have also written of the race in other novels and in a book of nonfiction called *Toward Positive Religion*. The race is my specialty, and I ask the reader to search carefully through this work to find the hidden meaning that is ordinary.

BOOK I

CHAPTER 1

A Brief Discussion of Television

The typical images on television today produce a show for us of biblical depth. One begins to wonder about the images, to find what they represent, who is seeing them, and where these images survive in the society. As television is the home of the image for the contemporary person, in old times, the Bible was the storyteller.

The question today, in the face of people from all walks of life is about the actuality of art. A theory of art may give us an interpretation, but for most of us, the production of a form has a complex existence. The actual meaning of constructs for perception, feeling, and thought, as well are appearances of various internal life experiences. The Cross of the Father is a perfect mark of art. The television is a stage for the drama of this religion, much like the amphitheaters of the Greeks. In this sense, low-grade Greek theater from long ago is to the variety of programs available as the quality of programs available now represent the Bible and other Christian holy books.

The Bible itself does not often appear on television. The book in its entirety, including the different versions, translations, interpretations and commentaries, as well as books containing references to it, not only could not be captured on tape but also could never appear in its original form. So the actual existence of the Bible may be perverted or destroyed.

The solution to this problem is to create an art of Christianity that may actually be exactly available to any person.

Christianity is well known for a capacity to create great art. The roots of these endeavors actually go all the way back to the beginning of the world. Since the time of Christ to this very day, Christians have expanded the truth. The truths, philosophy, beliefs—indeed, each of the absolutes of Christianity may be considered an art. In this case, art is any aspect of life we may choose.

Common forms of art are natural phenomena such as ferns, redwoods, hills, bays, and so on. These may have the most meaning to some people. Other common art may consist of actual behaviors of naturally occurring phenomena.

For example, the wind may blow a tree's leaves in a visually stunning way. The feeling of the bark on a tree for one's hands may produce a similarly amazing sensation. In rare cases of paralysis, or even for people in a coma, the natural experience of dreaming may be the art activity of the human brain. Verily, for each person, nature provides the essential reality of Creation.

According to science, the world came into being through a complex series of events. The human mind, we are told, evolved over time. At some point, people gained the capacity to perform various functions such as walking, gathering fruit, even shaping a spear. Shaping the tip of a hunting utensil or carrying fruit from here to there is a practical art. A few objects have been unearthed around the globe recently by archaeologists, who explain that the original people began to endeavor to begin with nature. At that time, we learned about fire, and the consequences of this discovery remain even for tomorrow. At some point, bowls were shaped, sticks were used to draw in the sand, and cave paintings appeared. The question then becomes whether humanity created art.

The answer is a definitive "No." According to the Bible, God created man and woman, as well as the world, plants, animals, and the stars. It is known that God gave us the power to choose. Apart from that, any other matter among people is debatable and almost always truly a sin. Creativity; appreciation; the use of symbols, paints, music, writing; and each artistic ability among us cannot approach the known capacity given to us by God; that, of course, is choice.

At this time, a significant number of worldwide problems confront us. All of us, without exception, will somehow have to go on through life. For a little over two thousand years, Christianity has pointed out the right choices for people to make. These have included the initiation of wars, leaders, priests, and people at every level of the society from farmers to carpenters. Many books on Christianity have been written, including doctrine, philosophy, theology, poetry, and novels, on topics of every conceivable possibility. In times such as these, with the expansion of knowledge, the dangers in the world require attention through easily controlled measures.

The Bible is a perfect means for this. I think I need not mention that it has preserved entire societies, refreshed the world, and even found new members all over the globe. The ideal of such a famous work may have sprung from the truth of the stories, the life of Christ, the Psalms, and the immense body of learning that has sprung from it. We know that great art has been inspired for centuries by the Bible, and we also know that it has sometimes been created amuck. Guidelines have been established at various times by the church, priests, and flock members to protect the society, preserve morality, and to continue to elaborate upon the truth.

The thinking behind many movements in the West in relation to art have been Inspired directly or indirectly by the Christian Church. These include, although not entirely and specifically, art after death in the areas where Christ taught and also the areas reached by the spread of His teachings. The element of art that relates to the purity of the Christian soul in connection with the Father may be one of the determinative elements of the quality of a particular work of art, a movement, or its interpretation.

Here lies the beginning of the intent of this work: in light of the chaos in Creation and the beliefs of the Christians, it should be possible to find a way to communicate the religion in a hazardous world. The question begins to form, asking, "Do we recognize the art of the devil when we see it, or do we recognize the beauty of God?"

The radical point of view explains that art is not a sacrilege. The conservative point of view may not actually be conservative enough. What is presented then is some medium for expression in which the dangers to the church are held cautiously at bay.

I am reminded of the recent attack on New York City. The image is clearly engraved in my mind of the planes colliding with the towers. The disaster appears to have been unprovoked. So why was America attacked? A scientific or a political explanation may provide some results. The fact is, then, that terrorists had the idea to fulfill the purposes of their madness, thus creating the events in the world that are still being played out. The absolute meaning of this disaster is not yet known.

Events in the world, great or small, do not gain upon us because we have the capacity to see or hear about them. To understand the art is to understand ordinary and painful things. The Bible is too long for most people to understand easily, while the sheer number of people, places, and events are not easily molded to belief systems. We may take the opportunity when we can to look at our lives from a particular Christian perspective, such as the angel Michael's, but it is difficult indeed to do so outside of a monastery or nunnery. This point should be understood very clearly; there may have only been one or two individuals in all of history who have been able to do so. Their names were Mary and Jesus.

The treatment given to the Savior is a personal ideal of the Father. That means that the message that he delivers is the perfect representative of Himself. The discussion explains that Creation is by God, art is a simple means for choice, the church works to save in Jesus's name, and disasters are difficult to understand. Furthermore, the recent spread of religion into different societies, as well as a powerful rise of distrust among the world's peoples, requires a new movement from the Christian Church to guide the flock members. The effort of this book should be but a small fragment for the future. To understand a little oneself is enough; the important point is not about our intelligence or some aspect of ourselves as individuals. Nor, say, could the perfect example by made by the muscles of the individual. Granted then that Christian Science has taken a foothold in the world, the next chapter should begin the initial stages of the art of Christianity.

———

CHAPTER 2

The Second Coming and Art

It is best to put aside childish things especially in a time so full of doubt and also in a world so fraught with conflict. Children are the blessed ones, and they should be treated accordingly. So we should believe that Christ would arise among ordinary people in the form of a little child. At this time, of course, it is necessary to believe that carpentry (the profession of the original Christ) will be reformed. In my opinion, that reformation will take the form of art.

The purpose of this second chapter is to describe in more detail how the art of the new millennium may be used as a basis for humanity until the Third Coming. In light of the fact that new technologies have been appearing in the world since the time of Christ, and that these have presented various problems to the church, we might expect that something similar will arise again after Christ is born, passes away, and life goes on. It is, after all, His life. So whether or not some new "idea" for humanity comes along in a thousand years much like science came along not long ago, the principles of life should be the same. In this case, I am presuming that the very old belief in "art" should endure and become a formally identified activity among Christians known as art.

From the beginning of Creation to the Old Testament and the birth of Christ to all the saints of late, a common cause, untapped, that has remained for Christians has been that of art. It was there long ago, as they say, at the beginning of the world, at the time of Christ, and it has persisted toward this day. Life is given by some knowing and the expression is the choice of belief for one who may believe that truth may be perpetuated as the life of Christ. This means that art is a simple medium for the life of Jesus Christ to continue, forever

Plato, of course, cited the preexistence of forms. A part of Plato's ideas stemmed from the belief of the Pre-Socratics in a group of elements. Philosophy, at that time, was merely an attempt to understand life. Everything in the world that has ever been is life, and nothing else will ever be possible. An instance of the preexistence of forms may be the case of the Greek theater, in which the individual knows the various degrees of drama by some instinct or already-existing knowledge. In the sense that art may represent life, and the philosophy of art is the philosophy of knowledge, the philosophy of Plato may serve as a definitive model for the knowledge of any form. Not only does this philosophy antedate many Western sciences, but also, the case could be made that the forms of Plato's philosophy were actually artistic forms, which, by their nature, made art possible. As one might easily surmise, Plato did not precede God's Creation; therefore, the philosophy really was quite radical for the time period.

Considering the powerful influence of philosophers like Plato, the divergence of the Christian religion confounds the doctrines of the human intellect with the appearance of the Savior. At this point, according to one's beliefs, Plato drops into the background for an extended period of time, while the church begins the long journey known as the salvation of humankind.

To avoid elaboration, the interested reader may look up the various facts and movements of philosophy and associated studies in the West. The important point is that in relation to the world now, Christianity has provided a safety net of religion that is easily accessible to the people.

The extent of the development of Christianity in the minds of most members of Western society has been facilitated by a number of factors. Among these have been political systems including monarchies, war machines including the Holy Wars, the employment of agriculture, and branches of the West one might see from any hierarchical analyses. Furthermore, as has already been written, the various disciplines of knowledge have been mixed with cultures. This principle of development has been a foothold for Christianity, and it is a part of the soil on which we walk. Western civilization has some sense of direction, from here to there, from wrongness to rightness, from immorality to humanity, and discrimination to equality.

Elaborations of the developments of religion in the West can be understood quite easily at this time. Children are known in the way of children, adolescents in the way of adolescents, and adults in the way of adults. The individual should have a few basic points of understanding, not necessarily by education, about very simple matters of religion. This may include cases of people who are born with a physical or mental defect; the act of walking down the street, lying in a hospital bed, or even just being able to move an eyeball connects the person to life. The relationship with Christ, the church, and religion is a slightly different matter.

Life is a part of the church, and the church has a say in the function of art.

It is important to notice that these three aspects of the world are closely connected. There are several reasons to find the beginnings of a system for art. It is produced extremely cheaply, in great quantities, providing the average person with a significant amount of things to think about. In other words, there is the perfect art of, say, the Vatican, the art of great people such as William Shakespeare, the evil art of child pornography common in some parts of the world. A second reason for The Art of Christianity may be described in our attempts to know about the sheer volume of literature, performance, paintings, architecture, sculpture, and each of the known areas. So in this sense, as postmodernism has proven, the perception of art is in the eye of the beholder. So whether we find the critical theory wrong or right, it could actually be correct to say that the World Wrestling Federation is really an amazing art, or that young six- or seven-year-old girls filmed in sexually explicit positions is art as well. Finally, life is not proceeding exactly as most people would like. At least in a democracy, this should depend on the people. It was the church that contributed so much to the survival and development of the West. This control seems to be slipping away. Of course, there are various other matters, such as the interference of different religions, the beliefs and art of the radicals, and other political systems, not to mention mysterious incidents involving drugs, lying, injustice, racism, rape, murder, betrayal, and hopelessness, and enough people know about these problems to prevent a correction.

Established in the world of Christianity, now, are systems such as science and politics, which seem viable. Changes in the fundaments of the society, at the political level or at the level of, say, accepted beliefs about the truth do not seem particularly advisable. How, for instance, would one go about changing the government of a country like the United States? The problems with this kind of action have actually been known for thousands of years. The Egyptians often had a very difficult time finding their Pharaohs, and their marriage practices, the primary means of ruling again, may have created genetic problems.

So at the various hierarchical levels of known systems, certain kinds of beliefs have been established. Interfering, again, in most of these social groups would not produce results of the desired organization according to the world situation.

I should not need to point out the difficulty presented by the international community. The layers of these problems are actually so extensive that even with very bright leaders all around the world, there seems actually to be not enough humanity to maintain world order. It is in this situation that we find ourselves, and without further adieu, the simple matter of a very crude form of art or communication shall be explained.

The next chapter will briefly describe the potential for various mediums of art to be realized as a method of sustaining the world. The reader must play along with the author, at least for a while, if only to present alternatives to the kind of speculation. Furthermore, in the reality of the United States, according to our own government, we have freedom of religion, freedom from oppression, the right to vote, the right to bear arms, as well as other freedoms. The fact that our country has been invaded, in combination with subversive elements, the dangers of war offer a chance to preserve a beautiful country and world, and at the same time continue with the experiment of democracy.

In the next chapters, the person of taste will probably find the writing a few degrees below the mark. Having decided while I was quite young not to become a priest, it is quite beyond my capacity to theorize about the Sistine Chapel, the churches of Italy, or the images of Mary and Christ on the Cross. The primary purpose of this book is to systematize the artistic aspect of the Bible and Christianity in general for the average American citizen. It is inappropriate for someone so young to watch television programs about difficult topics without the right kind of guidance. It is severely lacking in many families in America, and I think it should be clear that a harmless system that may protect children could contribute to the society while at the same time maintaining the laws of the country.

Similarly, for older people, the kind of stuff we fill our minds with, from too much bad news to some of the more elaborate explanations of morality, it is no wonder many parts of the society are headed downward. People can hear the right songs, do many of the right things, but in a much more significant way, they cannot hear that it is wrong to see the things around them that they see. If someone from the early part of the first millennium caught sight a work of art in which Jesus was eating human flesh from a table built of animal bones, what would it mean? He would reject most of us outright, and right now, how can we say for sure that we would feel any shame?

CHAPTER 3

Art as Principle of Life

Suppose that the eyes are a good-enough judge of art. What do we use in the endeavor to explain the world of Christianity to our children and to the people? One of the answers has to do with our holiness and our capacity to know truth through art. There are other answers, such as that it is faith that produces beauty, or that justice is the cause of worship. The point is that however we combine ideas, it is actually possible to paint the Bible, to write the Bible, and to express the story and morals in the most ordinary of situations.

A complete list of developments of the Bible in the world is not possible at this time. In order to point out the nature of art, other sciences have taken up the idea that Christianity works in situations such as these. For instance, a long time ago, the Christian churches themselves had not been formed. At some point, the various architectural structures were chosen, and ever since, the church has provided the way. Another case in point could be the alternative developments within the church body itself. Many so-called churches have arisen in the Lord's name, and this too has been accounted for. Christian Scientists have employed a special kind of prayer to the faith, and it is, of course, still quite a new branch of the tree. The paths of Christianity are extensive, and given the right chance, perhaps systems of thought will branch into each and every aspect of life. One may well consider the individual in Christianity and how their particular life deserves a book devoted to their particular style. Of course, this effort is possible and worthwhile, but the attempt to do so except by selected individuals would otherwise take too long for a single individual. Nevertheless, individuals wrote the Bible itself, and it has served as a perfect model not only for the Church but also for people of every conceivable race, science, and art. Interestingly, the race is well known for posing and being described by artists and scholars in the positive light of Christianity. In this sense, then, nothing should escape the philosophy of art and the greater denomination of the Church.

At one time in the Christian world, art was actually quite rare, at least art of a classical origin. Today, so-called art is actually in such profusion that it seems that the borders between the holy and the profane are difficult for many of us to see. Two questions then arise. The first is about whether the first painting of Christ was the best painting, and whether the second is about the dispersion of perfection of art deviated from pure sources. One should understand immediately that these words imply that the first words of Creation at the time of Christ have an authenticity we now call spoken English. Similarly, this line of reasoning may apply to all ancillary forms we know today. For poetry, a case must be made, for sculpture as well, and the laws of the Father will provide as chosen.

Art developed marvelously. We have seen the works of Christ's disciples in various forms such as baptism, the written recording of His words throughout history, particularly in the West. This has taken well-known forms. After a while, we began to explore, with routes into the East trod by such travelers as Marco Polo and others. At the same time, we were confronted with the difficulty of incorporating unknown religions, healing styles, and sciences. Their bravery and curiosity often brought them death or, worse, a departure from the faith.

To make a long story short, Christian art has appeared in different forms. This does not explain the purity of the church, but rather, it indicates that influences beyond our control have been invited into the public perception. Indeed, there was once a chance for the perfection of art, but events interfered in a particular way, and the results can be seen anywhere today. The historians of art are aware of the emotions of painters and artists, so in this respect, the research is relevant to matters of a higher order.

The time of the highest artists appears to have passed. The levels of the rat race have been overrun by a certain lack of discretion categorically, for the society to deliver a promise, the survivors of the art generation, members of the intellectual community, the ashes of the establishment, and the intention to persevere should arise as a Proto-Savior to deliver us from evil. The kind of person to fulfill the spiritual reality is the one whose eyes have not yet been seen. The eyes of the trust will one day close, the president will have to leave office, and among men, there is no guide in the world to whom the people can turn in a time of need. Politics are politics, farming is farming. During this period of the human race, those who can should carry us as far as they are able.

Consequently, in a period of great international change, the borders of the art world are ill-defined. The matter between intellectuals is one thing, and similarly, it is the same among the various groups loosely connected to the church. Of course, an effort to "restrain" artists will probably end in complex legal battles. Even so, the Constitution states that the president of the United States has the authority to lead the armed forces. Ironically, there are so few artists that a war with them would prove illogical.

Another line of reasoning might indicate that the television system reaches a potentially intelligent society. It is, of course, not the case that programming should change in such and such a way, with so and so appearing to explain the Bible. Rather, a system of perception under the protection of a known science, such as psychology, could make a few simple evaluations of relationships among the interpretation of images as they appear, for instance, on the television. So whether we are great lovers of the televised Sunday worship, children watching *Sesame Street*, or just an average citizen enjoying the World Series, at least people should be able to buy information with their rights respected.

Interestingly, psychology is in a period of rapid growth. The Hippocratic Oath of any good doctor, and of course the psychologist, should protect each individual in any situation. Although psychology is a young science, it might be possible to grasp the Bible in scientific terms in such a way that the relationship with the order of the day—i.e., television—can be brought into a safe house. This is, of course, a very tall order for psychology, or any science, to try to take up.

A fully developed science might have the capacity to attempt this job, and since psychology is young enough to be in a formative period, it should not take long to begin to describe the Bible in psychological terms. The discussion has, in fact, already begun. Feminists have discussed Christianity from several perspectives. Minorities too have begun to show up at the Table in the Sky not so long ago, and in the case of psychology, I think there might actually be a way to relate the stories of the Bible to the often troubling images on television of, say, families in crisis. Drama too is available for analysis under the psychological eye, as well as the variations on the themes we are so accustomed to hearing about.

I have heard a little about the famous people in the movies. I think it is actually quite questionable whether they are representing people of spiritual merit. The scripts on television speak too little of the way things should be. The identities of the Christians are kept secret along with the truth of the writers. The case in painting is that our freedoms have become the object of worship rather than the Greater Meaning that motivates these works.

An important issue among the people of this country has to do with the difference between the black arts and the art of African Americans. The exact causes of a great evil, like hatred, should *not* be allowed to run loose in the world. The meaning of equality and the practice of the Christian do not cross the line between the knowledge of the past and the appearance of an unwelcome guest. The society of artists should verify the existence of evil within its own midst, and the buying and selling of rare art should be dealt with by fire.

The way things stand now among the people, the immature and the weak do not have the means to evaluate most of the things in the world around them. So in this case too, the Higher Authority should provide, preferably in the form of the wisdom of the church, for the various sheep. After the 9-11 disaster, people of the Flock are beginning to wonder exactly who will lead them to safety from the Wolf.

In the case of art, some people act like wolves; others act like sheep; and the so-called smart ones, pigs, and disguise the world for their benefit. I have not visited a prison, but I have heard that it is a horrible place for criminals. The money in the world can buy houses for racists, but the hands of the people can afford a prison for people with no money to buy a house. The relationship among Americans is that their Hands are tied.

The art of the church is hard to criticize. The blunt minds of the people who fight are not always so blind. Turning on a television brings the world onto the screen. The president should choose between the availability of resources and the ability of those who use them. As I have proposed elsewhere, the church should find a legal way to elect the president. In a situation of war, the intellectual artists will fail if they try to outsmart an army. Science may provide certain answers, but only a fool would analyze the data as the churches were invaded, the countries were torn apart, and the children were burned alive.

To stop the invasion of the Western world from the forces of darkness, a simple series of steps should be taken in short notice. Other philosophers are trying to prevent the life equation from being destroyed. Among these are saints from across the world, the angels, a few groups of priests who can still be trusted, and the chosen leaders who must face the reckoning of the Savior as well as they can.

On earth as it is in heaven, so it is among the artists of the world that the leaders of the battles of the soul should find a place for expression. In common speech, this means that advertising agencies, video game builders, carmakers, and the people should take a place in the world according to their commander. The deaf can hear the music, the blind can see the paintings and read the words, the paralyzed can dance; each person with his or her own flaw may be able to work toward the greater good. Totally awesome, indeed, is the power in the hands of men.

The human world has a capacity for trust. The abusers of the trust should be replaced the very moment they are unmasked. The removal of such an American poet as Lawrence Fehrlingetti from the history books is not legal at this time. The great tragedy of life is not contained in pages of books written by prophets whose words lead to madness. The ghost ship of the prophets is not going to carry the words of the devil. The children of the earth walk a step apart from the path of a deceptive God.

Questions about the paintings of the ideal women stand outside the authority of the church. The rights of the artists are protected by the codes of the book. The human right to choose is killed by the immorality of an Insignia fashioned in an image of vanity.

The abusers of beauty may also be abusers of sexuality. The truth in art may come from love. The profane images show an art of enslavement to an oppressor of dime-store promiscuity. Unwed love disobeys the actual marriage of man and woman to the angel counterparts among us. The absolute sense of human love is not only unattainable, but also unknown in the perfect artist's imagination. Many people have heard a few words here and there, perhaps in a church, while the world we see is represented more and more like the world beneath us.

An Interlude on Psychology

A few years ago, I was lucky enough to be able to vacation in Cancun. At Christmastime, I planned to send postcards of the Virgin Mary, complete with electronic music. One of the postcards is on the desk where I write. I look at this image, and I see a seductive look in this woman's eyes. The psychology explains that women are often seen in a particularly submissive way. They are at once sexual and virginal.

Man is thought to be a little more of a problem. He can make "friends" with someone, and the beliefs about himself make him tell a woman he loves her. All he wants is sex, pleasure, and the feeling that his life is not a lie.

The human predicament is not just sexual. In psychological terms, people often say and do things to make up for the past. Therefore, we can explain religion as way of figuring out our parents. Our relationships do not obey moral laws; they are merely psychosocial attempts to feel better.

The postmodern movement was caused by a number of factors. Psychology, politics, communism, Buddhism, technology, the forces one usually thinks about in any given period. If we had a generic-type image for the situation in the world since the time of psychology, we could say that it was a period of great upheaval.

Art has come under the knife of psychology; in it, the glass an image forms of people whose license to continue to create is in question. The unconscious appears to hold some very dark secrets. The typicality of ordinary life, once so perfectly represented on the walls of churches, in the holy paintings, and in the look of innocent people's eyes, has taken the opportunity in the disguise of religions from far away to be known as the psychology of the deep.

The Survival of Greek Tragedy and the Church of the Race

Morrison has written truth of life for the church in the language of the race. Vonnegut, one could say, survived the destruction of the church since the immediate era of Christ. Few writers, indeed, could take up a challenge in a world full of disorder and hatred. Between these two, of satyrism and mystery of truth, the division between classics and Christianity may somehow survive. On the one hand is the period of greatest thought, and on the other, the feminine side, is the true name of Lord.

Verily, the art world is tearing apart the church of Jesus Christ. In the millennia preceding the birth of Christ, the thought in the West could be characterized as a developing form of hedonism. The seeds for philosophy, art, history, medicine, and many of the main branches of knowledge we know today arose. The gods represented the human world while the natural world was discovered to consist of elements such as fire, earth, wind, and so on. At about this time, Plato philosophized that the preexistence of form could account for the human capacity for knowledge, learning, and understanding. It seems that the influence of philosophy has not completely left the world of religion.

Toni Morrison expresses truth for us of a time apart. The Christian faith appears in her novels as a certain kind of memory. Time is told as a person interfered with by a man, or apparition. The Christian Church is not a grown-up place. The sickness in the world comes from leaving childhood, or the church, and meeting man. The roots of the younger trees reach back to the time even before the Pharaohs.

The uncorrupted art world appears to be heading down only a few paths. One of these is the classical style. The other is the perfection of the human race from the places where life really began. The oldest people in the world are the ones who do not fall prey to the evils of the time.

Art is, of course, uncontrollable. Television is dead. The Buddha cannot awaken the world more than he is. Even right understanding toward the dark path of nonbelievers. Art is, of course, not in great distress. It is probably wrong to attack different religions. In these matters of legality, science, or politics, I am afraid the matter is not totally under the control of art. Planning this part of the book is difficult for me, so some things should be left up to interfaith discussion. My mistakes in other books will perhaps one day be amended, so for the fact that logic is somehow a part of the thinking, some matters are better brushed aside. Nevertheless, whatever will be will be.

The French church, this time of year, I hear, has problems of its own. I have noticed that the peace movement is spreading around the world, and it may be viable at some point in the future. A book about peace is worthwhile in one way or another. It seems unlikely, however, that the peace movement will reverse the actual deaths in the wars that have been fought for supremacy, world domination, or the control of money. Perhaps the peace movement should have been stopped. Of course, the art of the French is often cited as the best in the world.

Italy has seen its share of difficulty. One of these is, of course, the fact that different churches have arisen from the land of Jesus Christ. It may actually be a serious mistake to think of the church as having split off from the truth. That is why the Vatican is the Vatican and not the Church of Scotland. The actual location of the Vatican, I am told, was chosen for its particular sanctity. Of course, I have only glimpsed it from afar. The more perfect the work of art, the closer it is to the divine.

The art world has come to be the way it is for various reasons. One of these is, of course, that in a free society, it might actually be quite difficult to stop the forbidden. Wrong art is not a usually a problem because of its material nature. Problems arise when the true beliefs of ordinary people are led astray from the most powerful force in the world, but many people appreciate it; even our thoughts can be artistic. When a little child cannot see the art of life in the right way, it will only take a few words for them to venture out into the fray. Children should be seen and not heard. Elaborations about a child's drawings are usually not to be spoken around a child. Adults who have a shot at art are, in general, no longer capable of failing the Christian faith.

The female sign has become a kind of language. How is it really, that men and women of the faith are different but speak languages that are intelligible to both sexes? Artists think about images too. The controversies in art are divided ultimately by the Spirit. Perhaps for me, it is a sin to speak of gender, race, and equality. Perhaps a language will develop, quite like the sign language of the deaf, just among women, or perhaps it's already there, and I have never heard the words.

The roles of women and men over time, we say, have "changed." The truth of art may not permit an end to human thought. There was a time in the world when Jesus walked the earth. The women of that time knew of a man. They called him Jesus. Did he understand them? Among famous people of art, do men understand women? Why do we know that Jesus did not have a female biology? It is said that he was born of a woman who had never slept with a man.

In relation to art, of course, the details of life are limitless. The evils seen over time between people, I am afraid, are unmentionable. A simple case could be made that says that certain people, or their arts, destroy all forms of thought or living. I remember not long ago seeing a report that explains that the forests and rivers of the earth were being destroyed. The culture of a particular group of artists somehow can actually destroy almost the entire world. The American Indians did not survive the invasion of the place where the white man came on a boat. The boat of the often-called Devil White Skins seemed to carry a kind of death. Now we honor the occasion with Thanksgiving Day.

Apart from the fact that there may or may not be a way to live among white people, the device known as the television could prevent a mind from serving the evil form of life. It is actually not possible to reverse a simple statement of life, particularly when there are so many forms of life. I am afraid that a television, which people watch, might be an obstacle to the survival of the species of the place. Explaining a phenomenon that makes vegetable life possible and explaining a television as like a particular word are both very complex phenomena. Therefore, in this instance, dealing with a perfection of plants seems almost as risky as watching television. The intellect may provide a thought about each of these, and a thought may seem to cause the people of the world to say something to the land. People of the earth are looking for an artist to match. The fact that destroying a place is risky does not explain art as a well as a taught subject.

A lot has changed since the time of Jesus Christ. At that time, the mystical aspect of His love was perfect and pure among people. Since then, Christians have lived according to the laws and morals of the church. However, the problems of the times have created a significant diversion for the people. It is difficult to explain the life of the world, but at the same time, one could admit that in the event of the Second Coming, the problems that have arisen among churchgoers can actually be dissolved by a very simple home remedy.

In *Toward Positive Religion*, I discussed the idea that God is the positive, and the devil is the negative. So in relation to a simple practice such as prayer of medicine, love of children, relations between people everywhere, and others such as art, the cures Christianity needs ideologically may be that our hopes in a positive God are restored. This may mean, for instance, that we take up our rights to live our own way in the world, while knowing that the absolute is in the human of all kinds. The common ground is just that—ground—and we all know the difference between an art and a ground.

For a long while, the best part of Christianity, as I imagine it, was the truth of Jesus's love. Now I foresee in the future a sense of the greater good. This might mean, however quaintly, that each person in the world may somehow choose something such as a positive life. There may come a time, when there will be peace mystics in place of where there were love mystics, more science mystics and child mystics where presidents once stood. In short, it will be any form of positive mysticism. Knowing what we do about war and peace, namely that it is wrong to kill, it is a sin to kill.

CHAPTER 4

Known

There is one known. The positive is the known unknown. Positively alternatively, the negative is the known unknown.

In the New Testament, there is a form of mysticism in the Book of Life called the division of Jesus into the souls of all men. The means that when He died, the Sprit lived among all of us. We can only imagine when He passes away again, how we will continue to know Him.

I have speculated about this a little. For what its worth, the world has reached a certain kind of way of thought. There are branches of other religions today that mistake a choice at one moment for an eternal choice to act according to a kind of law. Infinitely, we know, our lives are not just upon this earth. So our choice here is really only a choice here.

One of these religions, Hinduism, in my opinion, is the embodiment of the divine love, as well as it can be in humanity. Between people, God can make certain divisions. In this sense, then, ram, or Hanuman is the human embodiment of humanly divine love. In this case, however, we might feel that human choice is impossible. This reality may be like a scientist's choice to travel to the moon. To aspire to such a great height without a space suit and helmet is to commit a kind of suicide. The fact is that the Hindus are not insane about their religion, but actually, their souls are already going up to heaven on earth. The belief is one way, but the difference is another.

I trust it is not too much to ask to let the religions speak for themselves on these matters either. Perhaps I shall point something out. In the case of Judaism, the meaning is of the precedent among people for One True God. The second point for Judaism is also in the sense of oneness. This makes sense in two ways. One of them is, of course, the fact that Judaism appeared very early in the world. The second is that Judaism was the first to say that there is only One True God in heaven.[1]

---

[1]   I could say, at this point a lot about the religious leaders in our world so far. In the present context, I should say that Judaism really has the True God, but not the human embodiment, which is the absolute embodiment.

Buddhism is really very simple. I will drop the capitals on the Buddhists for something obvious. The Buddhists are, of course, totally compassionate. In my opinion, they could not even say that there was a higher power. The Buddhists are much more like doctors; they are doctors in the sense that their minds can bring about the human form of healing in the mind. Some of these say that people have a choice, and some say people do not. The Buddhists have a tendency toward logic, common sense, and the alleviation of suffering. I have always thought that this was not so much avoiding the wounds but dealing with the pain of the Savior.

Taoism, now primarily inhabiting China, is probably the most viable system on a major continent. The unity of dualism between masculine and feminine, dark and light, positive and negative makes for a simple small culture of the home. The world is actually simple, beyond the point of antagonism here. The way of living in the future is the small community, even to the level of the home. Taoism is an ideal form for the small community, and in this respect, China is the first country to rise in population above a billion and maintain the identity of the home.

The naturals of the earth are the ones who will save the world. I cannot say why for this; the people who do not systematize science are the preservers of the original way of life. These people have a chance to maintain the sanity against the nuclear threat. No one else can begin to protect our understanding of God's Creation.

This is an important point of philosophy. The presidents, kings, and leaders are not actually in touch with the meaning of the world. Only a person who understands the spirit of the earth can actually protect it. This is true of a few scientists of the West as well. The important point here is not so much our belief in God, but the understanding that the souls of all these people have already been saved and that any interference from the Christian world into the native cultures is one of greatest moral evils known. In short, this means that there is a true difference between the systematization of Christianity and the organic life of the natives. One might like to consider a Christian mystic of the Native Americans, the Aborigines, the Esquimaux, and so on. One should preserve the culture and life people without the oppression of Christian Science. I must say that if I had one absolute reality, it might be to say that Christ walks the earth now too as a native of some small place, almost equal to a rare native of intrinsic beauty. No ideal of Christianity should ever touch, change, or control the perfection of a group of the known.

On the individual level, there is some sense that one's human nature is singular. We may look into another person's eyes and wonder if we see the soul, the one. Naturally, we look at the world and appreciate you.

There is a problem with most of us, today, and Christ. The truth is that Christ is the one doing everything. He really does not want our negativity. He Himself gave us a choice long ago, but we have almost all come to feel that His Spirit is the way to know what to do. All of us are sick, and we ask Him to heal us. Actually, expecting Christ to do anything for us is an attempt to destroy the world with nuclear weapons. God is angry, and the second Flood in the world is in the form of fire. We should know that the right action is to take the choice away from Jesus Christ. The world believes Christ who walks among us is our personal Savior that we do not even realize who we are anymore. One way to go on from here is to take the responsibility of life completely into the human realm. Christ cares not for anything of this world, even we ourselves. To Him, this world is very much ours to control. Christ may actually be our true identity, even as we are born to a life of existence. Whether or not we manifest all of His qualities, our identity is identical with Christ's identity. If there could be only one Christ in the world, how might we explain the yet-to-be Second Coming? This does not mean we aspire to be the only Christ in the world but that until He appears in our lives twice, we may live exactly as the first Christ. I have already started the great problems of the world for the next generation, in my writing, so in a sense, everybody knows that matter and soul are problematical. The actual problem of the next generation is a long way off. This is not absolute. I am truly Christ, but not truly Christ II. It is a mistake to think that the First Coming and the Second Christ were and will be in the same body. In this sense, there are many ways in which my works fail all souls deeply. A heretic may think he is the Second Coming, but I am not the First Christ or the Second Christ. We are all equals in God's eyes. There can be only one Second Coming. Potentially, three thousand years after the Second Coming, there will be another arrival of Christ in the world among All of us, or an appearance in the world of the Third Christ, but we do not know God's will. The only reason Christ will return in the Second Coming is because since the First Coming, every human today has become him and known him in the way he most wanted. The Africans, the South Americans, the Icelandic people, everyone has reached the perfect state he or she was meant for in life.

What does this mean for the natural? It means that each human may express the absolute identity of Christ in any way he likes. If I worship the Spirit of the North American Native American, then that is really Christ. Similarly, if I worship Christ in the from of a non-absolute such as Mohammed, then I am Christ; in the same way that Christ has an absolute life, Christ has the existence of a husband wife, a soccer team, everyone in the world, and to each his own. We may talk about degrees of holiness, like a priest, a sinner, a frog, and so on, but the meaning of this is not possible for us to know. These ideas may seem controversial, but I should say that we know Christ was a man, and an absolute man. Men are equal. There can be only one absolute Christ, but we are partially so much like Christ that we may be partially absolute.

Further, that we are equals among men explains the diversity of belief in God. The Hindus, for instance, are absolutely equal to everyone too. The important point Hindu religion makes to a Christian is that God is among us in another form. It is the same with Muslims that Mohammed is God does not mean that he lives in a different class that Christ lives. It also does not mean that he is the devil or that he will go to hell. It is the same in one way or another for all the world's religions and even for the beliefs of each individual; individuality means that we are alive, that life has not left us, and that things are proceeding about as usual. Someday we will all be there.

There is some question about our home. Most of us have left home completely. We must return to our home. There is the house of God, or a church, but I think most of the rules and doctrines of Christianity today were not exactly done under the direct eye of Christ. This means that after He left His body, he actually went into the world again as a Spirit. This may be our Buddha nature, our food, our friends, and indeed, the whole universe. It is said that people heard him speaking for thousands of years. We could liken what happened to a drop of water dissolving into the entire ocean and finding the way rightly. The personality of Christ saves, while the personality of God among people is really known by the Islamis. If one cannot really understand that the Christ is the person of absoluteness, while the Islamis are the personality of God, then one should study a little more carefully. Christ the person is the absolute person, while we can understand from our sense of truth that the Islamic religion itself is not inferior; Islamism is actually neither a form of Christianity or of Islamism, and nor is Christianity a form of Christianity or Islam. The world's systematized religions do not create God, the leader, individuality, self, not-self, nature, love, compassion, and so on. That is not the meaning of life, religion, or humanity. Oppressing with ideas, religion, doctrines, thoughts, prayers, war, inequality, or slavery, or worst of all, in the way of a place, like the earth, is opposite the meaning of life. The meaning of life is to love. The warrior will die out as a race of all people. The meaning of the word "race" in this context is that of an individual with a particular quality or attitude, such as aggression, kindness, or humor, as opposed to a person with a particular color of skin. So in my case, at this moment, the race is the group of people writing the word "race." Actually the race is everyone, however they are, even warriors. When Christ returns, we will know that the world went the way it did with education, science, philosophy, doctrine, even flowers and plants to bring us to know the world in actual peace.

So what then is a home for God? Do we still call it a church? There is the greater home of earth, the home of a continent, or island like Australia, and so on. Then there is the small house, the place of the heart, the place of the country, where people can live in a small hut and live off of the naturalness of the earth.

There is a question of origins. Not only is the race divided geographically, ideologically, religiously, but also there is a further problem. Not all of us originated oh so long ago in exactly the same place. The stories differ, such as Eden, evolution, clay makers, wolves, fairies, fish, turtles, even self-origination, and the causeless. The sense then becomes were we a man and a woman in an identical place, or were we made of one another in another way?

Imhotep, a god of the ancient Egyptians, is not the only earth lover of the world who died out a little later. Particularly, in every part of the world, from small islands to the great continents and the poles, we know that there has been some way of actually loving and knowing nature as much as we love and know Jesus. The truth about religion is that it is a complex and varied phenomena, as different among people as it is among the individuals. Therefore, we are not only of Spirit, but also of nature, and in the symbiosis of the five—nature, race, individual, religion, and the land—one must know for sure, that there is a genetic element to the human race, with the Spirit, and that there is a reason the religions of various natural societies appear to have left the earth. These forces are still at work in the world.

It is important to note that historically, the Egyptians were the first to represent the world with an image. I think this may be what a television is.

Interestingly, the television is comprised of hieroglyphs that, in this case, is made of dark and light. We can see animals, people, and objects. At the time of the Pharaohs, the human language had not developed. As we know, the Judeans invented the number, which led to language in general. So at the time of the images, there came the numbers, then the words. As we know from the so-called freedom fighters, love is good to extreme of making all people equal. In this case, however, the religion was suppressed into the unconscious of the Native African. Now we choose to ignore the equality of life-religion. From what I have learned, the ancient Egyptians were powerful like the people of today. There was a serious mistake among the ancient peoples of the world in relation to violence, that we know for sure the African people no longer commit crimes without education.

There are many ways to try to face death, but ultimately, we must do so individually. It is difficult for all of us to lose a loved one. Oftentimes, people die whom we have only passed on the street, or someone we remember loving in a dream of all the people in the world. How do we know it is wrong to kill until we have done so and paid in some way with our souls? This is one of the questions of religion: is it not a greater crime to kill in mass, i.e., in a war for peace? As I have said elsewhere, the induction of soldiers into an army whose spiritual guilt cannot lie with a single individual, but somehow it is the responsibility of the Race and human religion.[2]

Occasionally one wonders why we fail to all of us get along. Isn't it a small form of dying to have a mean person there when we want a nice one? Whatever the case is with our desire, on the group level, at least, if we are all really mean, we will all die in a nuclear war. That is all.

---

[2]   *The Art of Peace*, Jeremy Scott currently unpublished.

Book II

Christian Practices in America

PREFACE TO
THE SECOND BOOK

One should forget that I have written in honor of the facts of reality in this world. The problems of religion, as I have often pointed out, have become global-nuclear in a cycle of negative reality governments. So in the event that I am chosen again to write a book on Christianity as intense as this one, I would like to point out that I was once a little bit of yippie. In case a younger generation is wondering what a yippie is, I will define that term. It was the preceding time of my life that brought the man, so famed for his addiction to the insanity of LSD, Leary, who named my generation "yippie" in honor of the gurus, Buddhas, and the other leaders and efforts of the sixties. On a personal note, one would say that physically, myself now being partially paralyzed due to spiritual suicide, America owes the world an apology for the use of nuclear weapons. It is the opinion of this author that that use was induced by the religious leaders who are yet too personally immature to appear in the world without trying to commit spiritual murder. The answer to this dilemma of life (as stated in the first book herein) is that all of the gods are really not dead. Italy and the Stalinese white man will not rise to power in the world again. If a divided world would like to explain this aloud through the leaders of the faith in public while also being known for it, they can try to bring themselves to say that they too have human flaws. Actually, and more absurdly, the wars that have happened are already over. They were not a mistake per se.

Logically, this author is under some belief in reality, safety, and protection. To continue this point a moment, if you will, consider that every known leader in the world has been executed spiritually, physically, as well as other deaths for thousands of years.

In avoiding the act of pointing the finger at someone in particular, the fact is that the worst trouble started in the world at about the time of the mass movements of religion. The continents did not meet each other until sometime after this. The worst calamity that still affects us all was the death of Imhotep. We should know by now that God will not die even when the human embodiment is destroyed and billions of people suffer, die, are turned away from their culture, and also react to protect someone who could possibly not need protection.

The Spirit of God moves everywhere and takes many forms. The angels of all the religions are now upon us. I promise as a Christian in the United States of America that they will never walk among us until the world is ready. How to you think it would make the holiest of us all, Jesus feel, if we destroyed his beautiful Creation over the fact that his infinites have always dwelt among us in many human/spiritual forms? 'Nuffsaid.

INTRODUCTION TO BOOK II

The Christianity of the Past

I will not criticize Christianity again. The absolute is too great to fight against spiritually. The wars of the past were a nice idea, resulting from the first meeting of the twelve major human races. A war is either internal, external, sexual, objective, subjective, ecological, emotional, personal. These may all have resulted from the formation of the planet, genetics, or perhaps it was a ferocious act of God. The nuclear holocaust has often been compared to the second world destruction mentioned in the Old Testament. God is asking the race a question about the Flood. No, we do not imitate him as a species and destroy the world with fire as opposed to water. As they say when things happen twice, "It only needs to happen once." After that, we can work it out. Perhaps God will try something different in two thousand years more? Maybe something different in between, something—how would you say this? Loving? Positive? Perhaps living on the human home that is earth . . . that is why I am against space travel. I would not like to deal with an alien form of religion, especially a destructive one.

In order to complete the tasks before me, this introduction will describe in brief the meaning of the years since the arrival of Christ in BC 0 AD. In English terms, there were positives and negatives all along the way. The human mind cannot measure the alternatives of reality. Of course, there are various forms of archaeology, analysis, and projection, when in fact the memories of everyone are genetic and depend on life. The reader should think that Christ will one day continue to be a memory.

There is another level to Christianity. It is the deepest heart of the human soul. People are granted a soul while they live here, and our nature is compassion in the eye of life. It may vary slightly among us, such as in the eye of spirit, the eye of nature, the eye of love; the qualities are many. Each of us has his or her own place to live in the way we are chosen. Our rights cannot be violated on the matter of religion.

Spiritually this means that the various dialogues between religions are failing. The problem is that the sources of life are all very small but one. I will not mention the only place known as the source of peace by name, but I think that before one leaves one's homeland, one should carry a lot less and think a little more carefully about what one is getting into. The meaning is that for all eternity the spirit of all of us in the world, even the wolf tribes, clans, art movements, education, and the future actions of the world. So the highest human right offered by Christianity is compassion with soul.

Whether we believe in the self-form of Christ or the not self-form, the physical form, the natural figure, the lover, the brave heart, the Judas, and so on. This will probably go on through diversity ad infinitum. It was the race in every way now, getting by.

I do, intellectually, know that it is quite a prediction that there will already be a permanent racial destruction by nuclear war. It is not as hard to say as one might think. This internal nuclear war will actually be fought underground in the realm of hell. Nevertheless, that door is closed by the perception of reality without gods present in some special way. That is why television was developed. It is the old voice everyone can hear, if she/he cares to try, of the world that was once thought to be the same for everyone. With exceptions, most of the natural world is dead too. It means that the human spirit used to see the drama in a rock, the dance of a lizard, a queen, or a famous actor. The television will one day be turned off by us as well. As all developments of the humans, they pass away, and we will probably enjoy the holograms of plants for the human desire to cause things to happen is deep, indeed.

The television may kill something of the natural human spirit. My own people, the Scots, died when we became knowledgeable. We used to talk to the dragons, the trolls, and the elves as the people of the world today really are. At some point, I think the Scots developed language and knowledge, like the others. We all know that England has not started a war in well over six thousand years. This is because the land is small, and the English Channel has not been accessible (except for us swimmers!) for very long. It is possible for us to defeat all forms of attack, including the nuclear. For the nations to stop and make peace, so that we may catch a glimpse of each of the continent's spirituality, is worth the price we are willing to pay—that of an active peace-inducing political nation.

I recently saw *The Lord of the Rings*, the old trilogy I read when I was a lad. The Icelandic scenery, where we originated, reminded me of something. Indirectly, one of our great trolls died when we decided to act this way in relation to so violent a world. In my opinion, a two-thousand-year-old Italian on his second trip actually had a great meeting in the other world. Of course, Jesus is the Absolute One, even according to the Jews, but the fight between them developed long before that, and this inconsequential matter of which of them has the right doctrine has already been solved.

Most gods have died, and in my opinion in the physical form, they can be tolerated even by Christians. The ideas remain, as we know, in various parts of the world. The form of Christ is preserved identically to the ones we used to see in the human form, the Buddha lives in his teeth, the compassion of the Dalai Lama continues, and on and on. This is not the central thesis, however; the important point is not only about the primary aspects of a particular religion. The point I wish to stress is that the very small aspects of the gods that were there before systematization are still inherently with each of us. The art of travel has stabilized among many mature people, and in the other cases, where the racial hatred is deep enough to apply to even the gods, the tragedy is explained by Christian Science.

This brings the topic of practice to the mind. Today, the world is significantly multicultural, and it is particularly important to pursue the survival of the human race internally. This does not mean that we should try to get the beliefs out of other people's minds, but rather, that each of us must make a firm resolution to work toward the altruistic aim of highest peace among the nations, states, homes, and families of the world. The vision through our window may be great, but everyone contributes to this act.

The tragedy of the death of gods is not only exclusionary to the Christians. It is noteworthy that many people study the classics. The idea that Jesus appeared on the scene and threw out thousands and thousands of years of their ideation toward the god(s) means not only that they had found the god of everyone, but also that they had forgotten the oldest lesson in the book. That one does not forget the angels. Jesus may be the highest form of God, but the angels of personality, ideas, art, love, faith, walk among us on the earth as equals.

The reality of practice has been the final state of religion after a leader passes. I regret to say so, the religions have become enemies in God's creation, and there is not a single chance for every individual to have the child's dream of him that we all once knew. Each of us may remember the walk down the path, the special meal, the race to finish, or some other thought that made us think. When we are children, there is no hatred, and only the adults can make it go away.

When we reach various levels of understanding, our sense of religion may develop. A very advanced woman practitioner a few of us know about in the West is Mary Baker Eddy. She took the hand of a new form of principle of Christianity that shook the fleas out of the upcoming attack of science on the religion. This has made her something of a missing person in the world especially after the psychological invasion of the '50s and the seemingly permanent disaster that we still know. Although her type of work is known, the possibility of overcoming the subjectivity of religion did not occur to us until a parallel between its own irrationality and objectivity could be made. One must never harm the life of subjectivity even in rocks or rivers. Typically, this is an absolutist language construction, but it is certainly the case that a form of oppression is death between animals.

Book II, then, will focus on the particular aspect of religion of practice. The introductory chapter will briefly describe some of the meaningful points of Christianity past and present. This will probably focus primarily on the historical aspect. It should be understood that detailed surveys are known. So a brief discussion of the meaning of Christianity and its shaping of the contemporary political affairs. The present state of Christianity in America is that Christ is present and actually walks among us. There is some problem of making past Christ present. As he does not speak for Himself, it should be known that the speaking of all the past can be projected safely into the aftermath of the Second Coming in the form of the renewed Christ of old living inside each of those who choose Him. As for the Virgin Mary, it is a serious problem for her to go into the souls of all people, as Christ is not her God, but her son on earth. Yet women have souls; their souls, I believe, are of their children. The question of the spirituality of a man and the spirituality of a woman are as incompatible as their sexual organs; their sense of language; the meaning of their lives; and, actually, their equality. For the attentive reader, a few more notes on feminism will be apparent in the subtext, psychological language, and theory of these chapters.

The focus here may be applied religiously to the other central figures of the other religions. Sufism, naturalism, Buddhism, Taoism, Judaism, Hinduism, and the various branches do not differ categorically as being the way of the leaders of human nature. Therefore, when a leader arises and takes up the power of God through an angel, such as the angel of personality, the natural angel, the angel of human balance, the angel of suffering, the human form of Y-hweh, the angel of human love, and the millions of different angels. It is one of my theses that all humans are equal and that we choose which angels we have in our lives, in the religious sense of equality.

The third part of the first chapter of Book II, dauntingly, is titled "The Meaning of Life." Titling the chapter in this way means that religion may explain this. The absence of evil in life comes from many sources, but I should say that it is not possible to understand the meaning of life. This third chapter is the most self-centered for this author; it came from a near-death experience in which he confronted Satan himself.

In the year 2000, two days after Thanksgiving, the author took the fall of David from the fourth floor of an apartment in Easthampton, Massachusetts. Though he passed from the world for the thirteenth time, the vision of hell was followed by a very brief vision of heaven. The author heard a voice from above from a bright light say, "Positive, Christianity." With a thoracic 3 vertebra split, and the tailbone in eleven pieces, the mind began to express something. It is still a mystery.

Life means positive.

The second chapter of Book II will deal directly with the art of practice. Among the seven main religious branches of the tree of life, diverse practices have developed. The highest practice is the practice of humanity. Attaining to the level of spirituality is something Christianity needs for the future. In other words, we might say that Christianity may stop to acquire the lifestyles and religions of the world, and start to know the absoluteness of practice. Actually, nothing can reverse Christianity; within, it should not have closed the door of practice-difference.

For many Caucasian Christians, this is a radical idea. The rationale behind tolerance may extend past the boundary of religious fear into new forms of individuality of the race. Absurdly, most of the world of religious difference could die within Christianity, should the religions that support the world differently be valued less than absolutely for their merit. The author is trying to say that love equals love in different religions and that the practices of them may meet on common ground.

Life is infinite, religion in life is infinite, and the actualization of practice during our lives may be known. For instance, consider a prayer of life: "Christ, have mercy!" We ask of him that we may pass through the world. We know that the morality of obliterating the Native American may have poisoned the world. The right way for us, now is to know that the prayer is as much an earth prayer for the survival of the people, or more. The Christian religion became a butcher in relation to the world when the church was systematized to the point of reaching away from nature. The majority of people at the time of Christ and thereafter lived in the church of life, a part of nature, and a part of love between brothers. Sadly, somehow, the mind of the Christian still thinks it is a sin to love nature, when nature is really Divinity itself. At the same time, the holiness of each person is not just holiness of religion, but of life. Therefore, that which is alive is holy, and there is nothing more to it than that.

For the subject to conform to Christianity racially as a form is mental and spiritual rape. I am a Christian, but I am not just Christian. Practically for the author, it means that the seven branches of practice are one within the world of love. So that we may not destroy the world of Christ, we may tolerate that Creation is made of religious diversity of practice. It is not my way. Nor may the realities of life permit us to know the world absolutely as Christ knows the world. For He Himself is a personality of humanity; potentially the body of him himself, old age may know. It means that the same thing twice does not need to happen in the world of women for us to know him. The practices in Book II, chapter 3 are about a relationship with the so-called other religions, which are actually seven prayers.

Should an individual speak Iroquois, that is Iroquois Christianity. Should the person love mountains, the body is the mountain directly, without the Caucasian ideas of the mountain. There is nothing in the human body that makes the knowledge of Creation Christian or non-Christian. We are already Christians-Natives-Sufis. One way of religion is the other(s) by human nature.

The fourth chapter will focus on the relation between Christianity and the Jews. The death of religion was painful at every step along the way, and the Christians are the guiltiest of us. We are all guilty in some way, but this conflict is important. While saying that we have no power at all, the Christians actually have the absolute power in their genetic religion. Religion is genetic. Like hatred, there are ways and means to overcome oppression.

It becomes necessary in this chapter to consider the possibility of peace between brothers. Is it possible for man to love and know peace in the face of the absolute? In one sense, we have had our temporary peace times. In another, woman is usually peaceful. The meaning of life is entwined with the meaning of death, and religion encompasses them both. The most important point here lies in the world religious situation from the standpoint of gender. The question is not why man will do what he will do—rather, is woman capable of evil?

The fifth chapter will consider Christianity and politics solely from the American schema. That political theory unbound from the religious context is unthinkable. It is known that life is religion and vice versa. The importance of a delusion in office of a singular religious-type leader is that he will fail absolutely to understand the capacity of another exclusionary religious political system in the world. Any effort to fail the global network on the part of a leader from inside a home of two to the continental capacity is not positive. The reality is that an individual mind cannot contain the minds of all the others and continue to lead. So the fundamental practice of a political leader for religion at this time is one of diversity. For the philosophically advanced thinker, one must clear oneself of beliefs. Knowledge is a form of power, but our claims of ignorance are beyond enumeration. The reader should know personally that the number of potentials he or she can use in reality is fewer than about twelve. The permutations within us of thought are known to disguise the reality of our own lives toward the same reality of other's lives. There is a human flaw in each of us that is known by each of us alone by the rules within ourselves that prevents the right way of life in ourselves from becoming known. The reader will excuse any conundrums in the language. One must limit the understanding capacity, the inherent person, to a bare minimum. For an individual to go above only several phenomena of mind will ruin him in the blink of an infinite eye, there cannot be anything at all.

Chapter 6 will confront a few thoughts about leaders. The principle studies will be George Washington in the political stage, the Christians in the American Native stage and women in the WWII employment stage.

Within the American family, a leader exists within each person. It means that there is an American will and that each of us who live here has access to it. The various economic, political, racial, and power divisions separate America. Americans, because of who we are, have the freedom to let the country slip. This is an anarchistic type of freedom. The best form of freedom for us is not the capitalist system. The best freedom for Americans is in the freedom of the people to pursue happiness. The ordinary life goals of us are motivated by the desire for happiness. The moral and conscientious majorities usually maintain America's freedom. It is the problem of religion and race in a free society that currently makes America great.

The footprints of George Washington in the political world of the experiment of America actually could not be a cause of the form of freedom America develops. He himself is not a model but a product of America designed in a planned rebellion by the world. American government was constructed not by great thinkers per se but that the world at large had a hand in its design. Most thinkers these days know well that even truly original creative thought does not outsmart the facts of history, life, and religion. In this sense, everything in the world is under the control of some form of historical determinant. The freedom of choice may be then understood not as an individual leader's ability but as the self-existing truth that one chooses for the sake of choosing. Remembering Washington's birthday has significance in the truth of the leaders that followed the first government, that connection is the identity of the American president.

Washington solidified a world dream of government. The reason he is important is not his political ability. The measure of his abilities is probably well known. The important point about the leader is the question of who he was in himself. Did he love? If the man who determines to try to fulfill a job literally is capable of reading and following instructions, the remainder will be his life as a person. What we know about him might tell us that he survived, that his courage was greater than his fear. None of us really knows about another and this means that the truth is in heart was probably not known. If he was not a man and a child, then he was not the leader.

The religious leader is then someone who inspires everyone in the world. It is a matter of attainment in others to the extent to which he brings the members of the race toward the sacred. These leaders in the flesh can be analyzed over the course of time as bringing their people to a height in themselves of profound religion. Their sense of reality is uplifting to the extent that people who find truth find the absolute, the infinite, paradise, the way . . .

Some of the qualities of these leaders are known. Only a few human beings could actually understand their humanity. This is usually the problem in the future as the leaders generally have a personal sense of vast periods. It might be best thought of here as someone who perceives the universe in a grain of sand, yet must remember his own name. We don't actually know; the individual embodiment may actually have grasped most of human history already but been so known even after thousands of years that he does not understand yet that people are mistaken about him or her. The problems with these leaders are numerous. In this chapter, I will describe a few of the problems not only in terms of the difficulty of solving them, but in relation to contemporary phases of agreement, disagreement, and the potential aims of the future.

Another kind of leader is the leader at the familial level. This person is known to all of us in a particular way and may actually be the prime form of life in our life. The parent or guardian is usually known by a child as the perfect figure. The meaning of this has yet to known.

The seventh chapter will be about the American home. It will include the relation to the society and the world of a small group, the idea that America is a home, and that during one's lifetime, America is knowable as a physical place. It is not yet known what the land really contains, but I believe that America is a safe place.

Chapter 8, a difficult chapter, argues feminism in Christianity. This is a difficult point. I have explained elsewhere that the art of man and woman together is more difficult than the cause of difference. Between such different people as husband and wife, brother and sister, friend and friend or foe, life and death, there is little known at all. So to determine humanity is not only about equality but also about everything in a woman's life. Certainly, a part of the situation of life and religion habits the truth of female.

In a very important, the female nature is completely secret. The truth about feminism is that it is and was a worldwide movement; the meaning of truth in this way is in its relation to masculine truth. There is a difference in believing in God and female knowing him in person. She herself does not attain for a reason so secret that one could say in her living form she is unknown to him at all. I will try to talk about this at length.

Another important aspect of feminism in Christianity is that woman is generally not thought of as a killer. There are several meanings for this. One is that a woman bears a child; she cannot kill to whom she brings life. In this sense woman, as the mother of a child, loves her children the way life knows life. Another meaning of woman's non-assassination is she could fear life as a life of her own loss. So a woman may identify the truths of religion as similar to her love. These types of reasoning are explicative of a nature that elaborates and survives on the grounds of a perfection positive love.

This book will also consider that woman is a protector, not a mother. This is a very important nature for her. It must mean that in her human person there are qualities that are internal. For a woman, the sense of power is significantly about nature as the knower of known female self. From her point of view, protecting the world is about the power of her difference to identify the relationship of protective to the nature of her power.

Woman is also pure like Mary, the Mother of Christ. There are various other arts, like that of virginity. Another sense of the meaning of woman is in the attitude of motherhood. Perhaps she is a perfect mental virgin in relation to her children. So in all of the religions, particularly Christianity, woman has a perfect reality.

A woman is more protector than Christ. This means that the attitude of woman is superior to man, though not in the standard of equality. In the world wars, woman's life suffered more personally than Christ's, as during other wars, though not in the same way in the religious field; Christ is holiness such woman is life.

In conclusion to the introduction to Book II, the central point in the following pages will concern the ideas of Christianity on the points mentioned. I should inform the reader that the meaning of these pages is complex and highly individual to the author. This means that the "history" is not the cataloguing of events, but a flow of ideas. For each of the chapters, the meaning is similarly mysterious.

CHAPTER 5

Practice is an actual sense of finding one's own way. Christ said this, the Buddha, as well as many other religious leaders. In Christian America, the world has actually become diversified in religion, and the pressure is very high to begin to try out the other arts.

Practice may mean many things and encompass a variety of activities. It may be prayer, healing, reading, study, church, Sunday school, education, teaching children, or the Red Cross. In fact, all of life is a form of Christian practice. Our lives, however, are brief, so there is some sense of specialty.

Because of a second coming or even a third, we may know that our individual life does not have the body of practice in the future. Therefore, the purpose of lives is not only to practice Christianity, but also to enjoy the world, to love our families and many activities. So although all of life is Christian practice, it is not also only truth that all of life is Christian dialogue.

The important point of Christian practice now actually has little to do with purely Christian religion. That is mastered by a few to varying degrees. The importance of the variances among practitioners is in two forms: the imperfect Christian and another is of the crossbreed between Christianity and other art(s).

There are problems. One of these is that it is very difficult, to say the least, to maintain one's subjectivity before Christ. It is an interesting point that Christianity is so powerful that many cultures often change, albeit toward the absolute, during the beginning of understanding of Christianity. Another problem is that the meeting of religion should have particular result(s). For instance, the result of combining the practices of Christianity with a different culture's practice of Christianity often concerns the ability, history, or inclination of the people.

A more serious difference of practice is in some known incompatibilities between religions. For example, Christ's doctrines of the absolute are not compatible with the name of the god-king of Tibet, Dalai Lama. Essentially, this means that for one true god, there can be no other(s).

So I might become a person who tries two practices, one of Christianity and one of Buddhism. I might lean heavily toward one or the other, yet the important point is for the combined practices' way to lead to the highest. It should be the case, of course, for someone trying many more religions' practices to find that way as well. This is probably the way for individuals with a political religious effect in mind.

The important point at this time is the aversion of the nuclear holocaust. In the future, I imagine, there may be other kinds of problems in an optical kind of difference. So our central effort now is toward avoiding seriously negative disasters, but maybe in the future, a kind of paradise door will open, and the nature of our prayers will change. It will be like changing the target of a bow and arrow to the safety of a hospital, not only this, as well.

The practice of the doctor is important for us no matter what is the religion. The patient is sick, in the soul of each of us, while our suffering may seem more important than survival in general. The truth is that in a new situation, the individual reaction depends on the best doctor. The failure of the nurse to control the patient is that she too must have her realization that the nurse is only so close to the perfection of infinity.

The political leader too, although not actually a medical doctor of religion, is actually a leader of humanity. For him or her, the responsibility for continuing such and such a life is about the reality of human life. He has the body, the religion, and the limitation. So for our leader of the country or town, religion is the absence of disease.

The art of practice, as it currently stands, has seven major known religions. The other five groups of the race are in a peculiar position to the twelve female groups. It is known that organized religion as it is classically known in the East and the West has sprung up around masculine identities. Known religion is masculine.

The capacity of woman to assent to these religions is a significant problem internally for the religions. Woman therefore is like a mother of religion who appears to the male form of person to participate truly in the religion. Clearly, however, the boy of the mother is protected by her for a time, in the relation of life, while the adult male grows to protect usually only his own people. Internally, savagery aside between males, religion is divisible in the world by two central groups of twenty-four-male and female of twelve major groups.

A more active practice of life, survival, love, knowledge—the various known reality factors is that of protection. Peace is protection, love is protection, life is protection as the absence of death; in other words, woman is positive as woman and man is positive as man. So in the human world of the difference of religion, the possibility of the continued disaster of religion may be resolved simply by accepting Christianity as the absolute for to tolerate difference by each person for peace positive eternity.

How then do multiple societies in the West, as well as in the East, proceed along the various paths of religious peace in the world now in lieu of the fact that since the dawn of religion life has been warlike at almost every level? Further, how do all activities of life aim toward the various goals over the course of the future of human history? My mistake, may it be corrected easily by the hands of the people!

As I noted in *Toward Positive Religion*, infinite practice exists, although not in the human life span. I felt blessed to have had the prayers and practices of religion in human history preceding my existence in the world. So the practice of religions of the world may be to bless children toward an aim of their lives. Alternatively, one might begin the practice of the future today, again, by praying generationally for thousands, millions, of years for the person to be born who will work in the world at that time.

Each of us may inspire another to find their own practice for today, yesterday, and tomorrow. This may mean something entirely original for my family as well. For another, the art of life may be a practice such as ten thousand purities. What this might actually mean, in a way, is that the reader must "fill in the blanks." It is, of course, difficult to write something down in this case.

I hope that one would try to find one's own way. This is one of the most difficult human tasks. However, there are other arts; one may conform because that is one's best. Often, the best way is to go simply, not to be original. I would suggest that there are infinite arts of Christian practice. Ultimately, there is not problem with Christianity, as it is the highest known art of love. In relation to other sets of problems, the highest notion imaginable is the absolute. Therefore, for us, the significance we gain in life in relation to God is best worked out for us in the meaning of our lives. Similarly, of one's life predicament is solid around the meaning, then the highest is the highest aim one begins to know.

Everyday life is Christian practice, but this is not only the case. The arts of study, the arts of mastery of various branches of worship, architecture, each of the known activities of past, present, and future are all well known for their relation to God. So whether or not we understand the doctrinal meaning of a thought, word, or deed, it is the fact that our lives are directed toward the highest knowable that contains the meaning of practice.

Prayer or devotion may release us from many problems. There are problems of sin; there are problems of selfishness, egotism, self-centeredness, and many other negatives of humanity. Practice may reveal truth, while in our human way, we also become positive. The art is to balance human perfection with the perfection of heaven and the other perfection—evil.

It is important to think carefully about the nature of evil. Why for example has the peace movement made it so far? It has happened in the honor of religion, but also in the honor basic human respect. So our ought is that prayers unify towards a particular goal, in extremely fortunate times, many goals. It is important, of course, not to let evil get out of hand. It is an absolute art to stop evil, while evil somehow is unlikable to us. Therefore, the art of stopping evil is categorically an art. The effort of practice continues.

In regard the evil of war, many people around the world join in agreement. In the *Art of Christianity*, of course, the effort is to unify all aspects of historical Christianity toward reducing the aspect of the known and unknown causes of war. It is the highest aim at this time, and in the future after peace is attained in the name of the Lord, the next aim of the world may be a further unification about another aim. I should certainly hope that by avoiding world destruction, the fulfillment is already planned for a similarly positive effort globally. Further, of course, there is the world situation beyond the world at that time as well.

There is a perfection in Christianity, and one should survive the nature of the life problems of religion. Because there are many religions, and because of war, it is necessary to take to the extreme the point of view of peace. The Christian practitioners have begun and now continue to alleviate the problem.

There are many varieties of forgiveness. One of them, and perhaps the most important now, should be one of forgiveness toward peace. The various known arts of Christianity such as prayer may actually be transformed toward peace. That is to say that purity brings peace, prayer brings peace, and so on. Reading the Bible should bring peace, as should reading this second Bible. Forgiveness itself is holy, and the holy brings actual peace in the world.

Actually, practice involves the whole mind and body. Every cell, every thought are directed toward some aim. To think is to practice just as to pray is to practice. Life itself is the art of practice.

The natural practitioner practices without his knowledge, and without being aware of it. The soul of such a person bears this mark. The important point, again, is to practice for only positive aims now and in the future.

So solving a single problem or negative emotion may take many years, just as thinking over philosophy takes a lifetime. So when we move our body, it is an art of practice (see below). When we breathe, we are breathing oxygen for the benefit of all beings. It is a blessing for us to bless the air with holiness and to make it a cause for life. We actually should not take breaths unless they bring actual peace by keeping us alive. We should not, however, die because we do not know how to go to peace. In other words, we get only as we give. So to breathe is to stay alive, and this makes this art and art of peace.

Taking a single step is taking a step in the right direction. We might say that planting our foot is rooting it in peace first for ourselves, then a family member, then for friends, then for the society at large, and then for the world. There are other arts of walking, such as healing a wound of war in an individual, sealing that person into peace with our prayers. There are arts of loving walking and virginity walking and the walking of protection by reciting the name of Christ. This may take more coordination than we have, but the important point is to try and never to go so far into a practice, a philosophy, or some aspect of life that we forget to call on all people everywhere and Christ to bring about real peace.

The art of writing too is an art of peace. We only write our Christianity for peace, to stop war, and to bring about positive prayers. Letters themselves, all of them, can stop wars; it is not so much that they are written in a particular way but, rather, that our wish is that they stay that way. Gymnastics, as I remember, is a gentle sport, and we should pray that all people will be gentle, that they will maintain the peace, and that we all should use our actual power, money, and thinking to maintain real peace.

CHAPTER 6

The Art of Physicalis

Circa 500 BC, physical arts of gymnastics, wresting, archery, slingshot, running, walking, sitting, lying down, mountain climbing, running the desert, farming, shipbuilding, architecture, psychological activity, elemental practices, as well as a full list. The Olympics had already evolved and the old gods of the West were all present. The relation of distance from each home of life differed as well as the meeting times of a number differential of potentially known actuality. Each known factor of life, to date, has play in these meetings, even until yesterday, tomorrow. It is in the here and now that the effects of disastrous war, fighting, and negatives, positives, pairing, and non-duality may be solved.

The art of Christian physicalis endangers the art of Hindu physicalis. Someone who tries this brand of Christianity should be well advised the door is left wide for a long time to the Eastern style. This chapter is based on plagiarism in a particular way. Not long ago, the author studied gymnastics and later tried physicalis. During that time, the author did not receive instruction from religious people at all. He read a few books. He would suggest that in all of this is very experiment and writing these pages, he had hardly tried this art in actual practice at all.

These practices have several purposes. The first is that they should bring about nonviolence, an intense feeling of love for Christ, as well as increasing positive knowledge of Christianity. As usual, there are many corollaries to emotionality, love, and the elements of Christian life. So in essence, the art of Christian physicalis is bringing the best of Christianity to the body. One might take a specific Christian text and practice releasing the soul into the body along with angels, the conscience, the prayers, and so on. This does not mean, of course, to eat the texts to get them into one's body. In fact, each of the factors known in Christianity that have been found above can exist here and now in the body.

Physicalis is an old science, about as old as Judaism. Gymnastics did not evolve into a formal part of Christianity per se, and the process of making peace with the East involves adopting similar practices. Within the classification of differentiated Christian physicalis there are differences between Christian individuals as well. Christians do not generally feel they are living an isolated island but, contrary to the point, feel that they are powerfully connected to Christ. Because there is a connection to the soul and the body of the individual, there is a connection between the body and that to which the soul is further connected. In this case, the ground of being is something real too, like the body, as well as the sun and moon, universe, and God. So for subject, the subjective soul in the body is the proving ground for all of God's creation. The body falls not into the field of disvalue. Rather, one could speculate that the body is as valuable to God as the entire universe is to Him.

Treating oneself and others without violence, harm, or disease is one factor of reducing war in the world. One art of Christian physicalis is that of peace. Another art is known Christian physicalis, or exercise. Science and health include a discussion of healing principle. Other principle is known. The body, soul, Christ, each attribute of being is known in Christianity. So Christian physicalis of known has all the attributes of the body and the universe of God. The diversity of God's Creation is called the many; the similarity between the many and the many is like none of difference in the many. So from this perspective, God's Creations are all one. At some point, long ago, the world was Eden. At that time, Christian physicalis today is to find the peace of Eden. One hundred percent divided by all Christians is saved like money for the positive of the future. Christianity of the future is infinite, eternally infinite not to lose against. He will choose, but not for no one to lose. For some of us, Chrisitan physicalis is knowledge, like in the garden, yet there were other relations there possible. Such as science and religion.

With every practice, there is every known, and in each practice is each known. This is the within of the Christian soul's Christian physicalis. Within each is each, and all in all, the object known to the subject. Arts of physicalis are meant to maintain ground against the various calamities of each person. So regardless of what happens in the future, the point that we must adhere to is the known. The known is actual peace, just as the body of Christ is really actual peace food and drink.

Realistically, the author knows that this is risky thinking. In Scotland this Christian art of physicalis is actually the art of Scottish worship. The difference between the two is primarily one of ecology. The Scotch Irish and the Nordics cover Christian territory like the others. However, based on the location of the people of the earth, the climate, food, drink, and lifestyle, our experience of life are actually quite different. For instance, the African territory has many more fish in the sea and is in a different relation to Italy than the Hawaiian continent. It is similarity between South Americans, the people in the Caribbean, and the Japanese Chinese. No inequality of failure, pain, loss, gain, love, positivity, and other traits as well. Christ is everywhere in the here and now, and then he may live again, in new form.

The Christian art of physicalis is not permitted to employ the object of mind of simple intra- or interracial spiritual nature known "that" or "this" of object nature. The reason being is life subjectivity positive knowledge of peace. Compassion Christitam art of physicalis positive. Obviously, the current mind of Christians knows objects in the world. For this basis, external person's objects are peace positive. Elementally, the world is old; in this sense, the here and now is old, newly, like newly old.

The art of negative and positive and the known do not match identically toward the elements themselves one world. The mind in the long run in the here and now, soul in the here and now. The angels and the conscience here and now as well. So a negative principle (not negatively evil) has the potential for physicalis, as well as the positive (not positively evil). So negative and positive can mix. This is not, however, the way we actually experience body-soul, body-soul-conscience, and so forth. Usually we know our lives not solely in terms of positive and negative, but in such terms as "the prayer works," or "the Virgin is broken." So for this, a prayer for peace made of Christian physicalis or the body cells of the entire person are Christianly virginal. Not only do positive and negative meet herein the body, but also, importantly, physical elements of constitution. So we are comprised of life elements as well as the food we eat, the air, the sun and moon light, trees, the earth, starlight, everything, all, each, singular, many, words, prayers, our parents training. So the piety, Christian nature, racial nature, knowledge, intelligence, trust, and others turn the positives of the person within, just as the soul in the body is still one hundred percent soul, and as God turns the universe with his bare hands.

Establishing the meaning of Christianity as a reality within the body is to say simply that the Christian Art of physicalis is about nonharming, nonviolence, and peace. So many qualities of the soul actually spread out, so to speak, into the body. This may mean many things, such as that the soul is focused in a particular spot, but in particular, the important point with the powerful soul is to let the body control soul by the body. Of course, this art is not for everyone, and for each step along the way, there is a corresponding art. Simply put, the body is the person, and the soul may only remain in the world with the body.

Knowing that the body in the mind of God is somehow spiritually eternal and spiritually infinite, then might it not be the case in the here and now that the only thing that actually matters to him in person is the person? In this case, the person contains everything of God, while the body, which must die of old age, by peace known.

So walking is an art of physicalis, although a minor one, while serious descendents of old-time gymnasts, wrestlers, etc., might begin to ask themselves exactly which positions of the body one actually tries to put oneself in.

There is a technique of prayer in the body in which one imagines the cells in the bloodstream bringing healing to the person. It may bring quite a negative state of mind, particularly since prayer in this system is spelled "here and now."

The cures this miracle works have to do with where you really are. So the prayer is spoken aloud: May peace come to us here and now, wherever the others are, especially since they may need our personal help. When the prayer, soul, life journey of the here and now is made, the self begins to find ways to aid people. This means that under one's religion, the feelings, thoughts, and emotions are communicated via that communication within.

Here and now is the place we begin. It is like when we open our eyes and were born.

The body is in the present tense. This may mean many things as well. For instance, we may think that the virginality of a single-cell moment's virginity is the virginity of the other cells. One must not try to think, as the thinking faculty is a party to the mystical soul.

One must think the soul equals all things and people, animals, and plants and symbols, truths, love, being. God's grace can enter the body through peace for peaceful aims. Without the body, God's access to us is limited. Christ of Grace goes on through us, but through peace and love between people. Here and now, where we are reading this book in the present moment, peace is possible, and in the here and now, it is the key to beginning an infinite fresh relation with Christ. He who favors angels of God can find them here and now as well. We are not, as Christians, designed to have much. The sense of "having" got very out of control in major parts of Europe and, more recently, the North American Hawaiian-Caribbean continent.

Important questions about the soul in the body often take complex results. One of these, and the author's own, says that intelligence is identical with the soul, and that also so is the equality of the minor human traits. The equality of the soul is wondering soul here and now is equal known. In this case, Christ's actual physical body had the Great Soul of God. This we do not have, joyful, sorrowful, all knowns, and somehow the body of the individual He did not forget. The pain we feel is indeed to be remembered by ourselves, and it is notable to remind ourselves to treat each other with the trust Christ deserves for us to remember each other by.

A simple way to start is start with the simple. In other words, find a quiet space free of obstacles on the ground. It is particularly suitable to start out in nature. One might like to take a walk to think over nature. In a clear space, focus the soul, usually situated in the head. The soul should fall silent after a few minute. The position to begin with is standing. The first gesture is the hold the palms together in prayer at the level one would usually cross oneself. Hold the position a moment, and then move the hands in the direction of the cross. This is the first gesture and may be repeated as often as one likes, even sitting, lying down, or in any safe way. It symbolizes the gestures of peace, love, compassion, in the form of bringing oneself to the here and now in Christ's name. The beginner's art is the art of freestyle. So to avoid the physical problems, the art is to find one's own way physically. In this regard, I will only describe a few assumptions of the body and leave the reader to find, even simply, a way to sit, lie down, walk in Jesus's name.

So at that time, when one has finished Christian freestyle hand gestures for peace, one should move the body into a suitable position for the soul's reentry into the body of his Creation. During this time, one should think only positive thoughts such as Christ's love brings actual peace, compassion, endurance of personal difficulty, charity, giving, and other qualities of angels and saints as well. One might experience a dream at this time about Christ, or a particular angel, or God himself. Falling asleep is not a problem, although staying awake is best for exercising.

So at this point, after moving around freely for a while, one should think of the way to let the soul enter the body and permeate the muscles, nervous, bone, brain, eyes, ears, nose, skin, feeling, hands, feet. Relaxing might be useful, while maintaining the tightness of the various internal and external body may actually be more positive. The important point here and now is to let the soul and the various facets of Christianity move as they will within the systems of the body. It is very positive to have faith at this time in the routine to allow the angel of disease to enter the body and move freely through the system. Angels do not kill angels, and people do not disease people. It is the principle of nondisease nonviolence. In fact, an expert in Christian Science already adopts the body. The soul and God may move therein as they are.

One should know, of course, that the art of Christian physical is not to attain physical slimness muscularity per se. The example of the ideal body shows little in relation to actuality. The people one knows behave physically a certain way by soul in body. To influence another negatively or positively is not known. Similarly, to act on another with the good of nature is positively not known, and to act with evil does not accord with prayers for simplicity. Negativity and positivity do not abhor evil in themselves, whereas neither do positive nor negative equality evil. The meaning of the words is surely simply different. The body is natural by any standard. The Christian art involves natural. The positive is natural, the negative is natural, and it is wrong to kill a human body. This means that one should practice with the body to release a difficult birth by prayer of the soul rather than try to defeat the beast in the embodied form. So the world, or the group, unites for peace to save a single individual at all.

Jesus, the person, lived an ordinary life. He lived and died in his father's name. The important point to remember is that as who he was, he was known so that he is who he is. So in general, we are ordinarily aware of the body, as Christ mortally was aware of his. We may wonder, was Christ aware, in person, of the future, such as our own lives? Knowing humanity, no, he wasn't mortally aware of the future. It has nothing to do with him avoiding his death or assuming so.

The art of the soul not leaving the body until death by old age is the true art. There are other methods to fulfill, but one is that one's practice brings death by old age to all other people. The practice, therefore, is one of ending fear and negativity of all kinds. One might consider this practice positivistic, but in reality, it's merely the human art form of employing the body in worship. The body becomes the church, the love, the compassion, and becomes an expression of Christ's qualities. So to really love him is to love others, by the art.

The soul may be subjective, and in that instance, the already subject one has the soul in the body for life. In this sense, the soul is changeless and subjective, whereas for objective peace there similarly implies no harm, no limit to the soul in the body. Without conscientious peace in the body and soul, one must identify with the peace. Peace is every soul, and the body as well. The conscience has awareness of morality within the body. To know for sure that another remembers peace in all subjects, in person, right here speaking to another, actually trusts the other at the price of the unknown. The important point is not to suffer or to cause suffering within or without the body at all. In fact, the less self-centered the soul and body become toward others, the greater the likelihood that the individual will become healthy by peace. One's courage may increase by "taking" a disease from another and employing the art of Christian cancer physicalis to cure it. The yogic art of specializing increases as well during the time one's soul chooses. This art of Christian physicalis should choose to either be diversified or specialized. The author expects the reader to learn for true the physical arts of Christianity from learning or from prayer. In this aspect, the important point is to make small physical choices in the body and mind, and to center around one major choice, but not to choose over and over.

The body, as a Creation, has a perfection in it of God. That tells us the soul has been making us walk all along. So the body has its own causality, and in the soul, there is causality too. So from a very crude point of view, the body is actually very subtle. The twelve symbols of the world is something. To know that one attains a variability in general, in the body with these is, of course, to know the wide variety of religion style. As noted above, Christ is the ideal Christian, and to try to attain is egotism. This is not really moral egotism, but egotism that Christ's spiritual nature is imaginable except in the Second Coming. I believe that during this time, he himself will not leave a mark on the world. The world should make the prayer that he should not be known to others much at all, but just that he may live out his life in the peace he wanted. This prayer is the world's thousands of years of peace, and may it be made so.

The body has receptivity. Like listening to music, receptivity is closer to peace than activity. The feminist art of receptivity does not emasculate men. The art of masculinity is the art of Christian peace. The infinite art of peace contains all things, and people are one, yet not one, many yet not many. This is not only a sense of difference, sameness, object or subject, opposites, like or dislike. The true art of Christian physicalis, not owned by anyone in particular, specifies the art of functionalism.

Physically, how is the art of relationalism? In person, in body, with our souls therein, relating to another brings peace. The words and tone of voice we use may be bitter or sweet, Chinese or Maya, same or other; the important point makes known peace. If necessary, one prays in person using one's whole body to escape, say, an aggressive drunk.

The physical arts are nonaggressive. Strength, receptivity, trust, honesty, and love fall into the brackets of religion. Religion is generally positive; however, human nature is generally not responsible enough yet. It means that the Christian society needs to slow to a stop and turn toward peace and great positives, in the world, particularly in person. The body here and now is the soul in the body in person in the here and now. The author will disregard any claims that he himself knows anything at all about solving problems. The author has noticed that various evil techniques have developed in the past and present for violence and disease among all Christians. These have often been followed by society-wide deceit. The prayer is for the cessation nonviolently even down to the least thought, feeling, cell, DNA and RNA, of peace by the final silent door of negative angels closing in heaven.

To find a balance between evil in the positive and the negative with the body and the soul is a critical point. The earth of people is currently in a critical balance. There are strong and very old balances. They may be long-lasting, and the world wars are too young to attain balance. The Chinese, for example, have symbol grammar elements of balance for a long time. Somehow a balance is possible in Christianity of the race, for us all to know the natural balance of peace by simplicity. This is food, house, and survival until old age. In the difference of many among several main families in particular the Nordic race, the Italian race, the Hwn, the African have the key to this balance of the cross. It depends on the very roots of the various meetings of these people. We must find a way to make peace. Perhaps it will involve giving the trust of food, shelter, and a belief of mutual differences, similarities for surviving until old age. I do not specifically mean leaders, as everyone in these groups must eat, sleep, go to the bathroom, and live in such and such a way.

The soul thinks or the thinker is the soul. So are the soul's thoughts in the body? Are the leaves we eat in the here and now in the soul? Subjectivity may be the soul, or the objects of subjectivity to see in the soul. Our very person is the soul, even in the form of subject, or the deep aspect of mind, intelligence, belief, trust, defiance, respectability, stories, all of these are free soul in body. As stated herein, it is free as it is based on the primarily current activity of humanity, peace, whereas the more expensive the activity of the body seems for peace the less peace it actually is bringing. That is a subtle form of economicalism. One does not eat money, one eats food for peace.

At this point, the soul is nature in body. So any form of subtle body-soul involves no violence. To the contrary, as subtle forms of love and peace, understanding and trust gather in the body through the connection to soul above, the self begins to become more ordinary about the world. The body is made of the same stuff as the earth, the animals, and plants. The sunlight helps the plants grow oxygen, and the earth provides minerals. Water flows in the ground for the trees to make sap, which, with sunlight helps to change carbon dioxide into oxygen. The principle of consumption is the same. To cure cancer, we do not eat ourselves. To solve a problem we await an answer. When we are hated positively, the negative balances with the right ingredient. A blessing in the soul makes a friend even in difficulty. For each thing, there is peace. The important point is Jesus Christ's family, his cousins, aunts, uncles, whatever the color of their skin, and especially their freedom from war. By subjectivity, the world of the body, is the world itself, yet we experience different *and* same; this means that each source in the world is peace. The true cross and the other amazingness of the other people.

The author hopes that enough information is begun for the first years of Christian physical arts, and for later years to start afresh in the time of infinite peace.

The art of physical breathing toward the positive soul springs from the sense of the wind. The wind has blown since before man and woman, and the first animals needed oxygen. The first man and woman breathed air, and it supported them. So to take the breath helps keep the soul in the body. The breath strengthens the connection to the environment and to life at large. Plants help to make the breath with the ground and the clouds sky, rivers, and oceans. To accept it as a very simple form of the cross is also to accept all people the way they are.

So the body keeps the soul with the breath too. As one strikes poses, one watches the breaths. We watch the breath because it was breathed into us by God. If we are careful, the physical art can pull us back to the garden. Life is a garden, and we breathe in this garden. So to take the breath is to remember all the doctrine of Christianity. Breathing simply keeps the mind and spirit in tune with the body.

This physical art may be practiced for any number of reasons. One of these is to preserve and increase the virginity. A second is to increase or maintain purity. The reasons these work are simple. The body is the place for all of these events to happen. Instead of the Holy Communion, we can do these. The soul's magic applies. The soul, the vessel of things holy in this world, adds to body a new dimension now. An angel entering the body will bless the body, but to achieve the aim takes practice. God Himself may dream of our bodies and try to help us through our practice. The art of gymnastics is really an art of Christ. The writer is sad to say that sexual accidents sometimes happen without an instructor, particularly during the first few practice sessions.

As the soul circulates through the body, the principle of physical art moves through the bloodstream. The blood passing through most of the nervous system and internal organs is moved by the heart. The heart, symbolizing love, keeps pumping. These practices may extend one's life, even making possible the rare art of sex and virginity. The art is possible here as the physical motions of sex restore virginity while it is taken. It is very rare, and the author recommends against experimentation. The female's torn body will heal, and the male's mind and body are restored too. There is a particular position for this to happen during intercourse. The activity, mind, prayer, and reading of the Bible in the mind will work. The art of negative pleasure should be treated in absentia.

The practice of health is somewhat different. In the art of gymnastics, the healing principle of the cross is taken. One lets the healing energy move through the body. At first it is the whole body, then parts, then cell by cell, and finally, living atom by living atom. Each movement strengthens the body, mind, and love of Christ (or particular angel).

Knowledge enters the body too. The mind and soul have a peculiar capacity to involve themselves in all activity in the body. The body is the temple, and the soul is the worshipper. If fact, each element of the world above enters the body. The body can cannot and can't not show virginity by this physical art. There is some sense of risk the first time.

The here and now drops into the body in the form of various holy symbols. The cross, the stars, the sun, trees plants, all of creation. Gymnastics creates the energy of any Christianity, or an art thereof. Actually, any form of worship may be practiced.

Alone prays, and the angel becomes the one of knowledge; oneself worships the cross and intelligence becomes the known of Christ in the body. All of life lives in the body, and is the curative force of gymnastics. The woman and man who make love become husband and wife. The cup of life holds the perfection. The angels born in the world are born thus.

Physicalis is prayer. The nervous system adapts to the soul while an angel may replace her. As the virginity increases purity, faith, trust, love, understanding increase as well. It is best to increase only positive potentials. To the brave practitioner, he or she may try to make leaps of faith while practicing. In this regard, he or she may try to increase bodily things of good and evil. The risk includes that he or she may get caught in the body on the problem. If this happens, he or she should pray diligently the old-fashioned way.

One of the arts of physicalis practices to find one's own way. Quite literally, this means to work with one's own body postures, exercises, and motions of the soul. Otherwise, one conforms to the postures below until one is ready to think a little more for oneself. There is nothing wrong or right about either of these; they are both just prayer and worship, trust and love.

Again, the art of virginity can stop the sexual function by the practice of physicalis. This is actually an overstatement. What the author intends here is that the physical art can can the cessation of the desire for sexuality more than other arts. This involves the nervous system, the internal organs, and the rest of the body as well. The practice is the same. However, the angel of physicalis acts in unpredictable ways. As I learned this practice, I felt less and less in control of my body, but more and more finely tuned to the realities of Christianity within. So a part of the practice has to do with the angel, while another part of it has to do with the body. As virginity increases, the body may react strangely. For a man, his seed may spill spontaneously. This is an art of virginity.

CHAPTER 7

The Art of Christian Emptiness

Emptiness

Christ had true nature. It existed in several ways, and they are important for the meaning of the absence of self. The first is of Christ the mortal. He Himself was wholly human, no more so than anyone else. Granted, he was the son of God; at that time, he ascended to a level of human understanding in relation to the Divine. This is his second nature. He was so fully developed that the quality of his mind "took" the absence of Himself from the world and replaced it with love. This sense of absence with him so completely cured the world that at that time, this secret went unnoticed.

So Christ completed the world with love, compassion, and peace. For him to take the positive qualities denies the exact sense of what really happened with him. It was, and it still is, a mystery.

This was not the only absence Christ filled up. Our knowledge of the worlds of heaven and hell actually was realized at that time. So the revelation of the world above and the world below developed after Christ. At that time, for Christ, the Absolute One, he chose desire in general to fulfill himself in the name of God. Desire, however, may be understood as the absence of none desires. So in the case that one chooses something new, it takes a long time for things to change, as He passed long ago. Generally, desire as the cause of suffering takes other attributes. In that case, the approach is to see desire and suffering as Christ's friends. Writing ignorantly, if there is an angel of peace and an angel of mercy, then there is angel of desire. In this context, the angel is Christ's alternatives to desire, but not the relation of desire to suffering.

To explain, Christ died for our sins, and it involved physical and mental suffering or pain. Perhaps it is best to remain silent about sin, but the author might add that suffering is not necessarily a mark of sin. It means that when one's feelings are hurt as a little child, the mental formulation of peace greatly outweighs the physical sufferings of the world. As noted, the physical and the soul are eternal, yet one may suffer on earth. So in the absence of love, the cause of Christ's peace exists solely in relation to choice.

To explain further, one should answer as to the way the mortal soul answers absence in himself. This has to do with Christ's tendency to care for each and every person, animal, and plant. Christ cared about people, and we too care about people. Even if we don't care, we're people too. So within ourselves, we do not attain to Christ's full nature; all people experience known of people in caring. So our small caring is the caring of the same nature, in the same way that Christ's nature was loving. So our mind may not be truly absence, but people notice their nature in the soul of causality.

In all of human nature, the soul elements are the soul elements. I sometimes wonder about other religions and what they believe. This wondering is important. It takes us back a step from the intense involvement with too many others in the not here and now. To reach true wonder in the here and now is to forget what we have been keeping our soul in, and to move farther into our present life. We may feel we are, and always have been, full, of the Christ element in the here and now, but the love we feel is really meant for us to know others by. God created a world of peace at the time of Eden, while the here and now of lives might lead us to the Garden of Eden in the present moment. This brings true life to our souls, our friends and family, and to the greater peace of the world at large.

In the here and now, the soul maintains the connection to the body. The not here and now has the soul while we live in the Creation of God. The Creation of God is immediate, present, and infinite. The vision of Christ is in the not here and now of the soul, which is present where we really are. So the absence is the place from which we came to be here, and Christ's love is what we know in other. The intellect is an obstacle to love, and the difference of intellect in the method of the here and now is the same. Again, the primary place of the soul is exactly where we are there at that given moment.

What is the here and now? Where we all are right now. The important point is that our absence does not exist on the people around us at any given moment. It means that if Christ's love comes to us, we should know that it is our own capacity for absence that invoked it. It should be extended to everyone, whether or not we want them to be our friends. It is the same with compassion. We have the capacity for our own compassion too, and it is this that invokes the compassion of Christ. The highest absence is that of Christ's actual peace. When we find the causes of peace in actuality, at all, we make it known in the here and now, freely. So in the here and now, look for the causes of actual peace in the world, now and in the future.

Christ's love is truly blissful. To know something simple, like a friend's words, a room with a window, a walk down the path of Christ, a view of nearby garden, is really the simplicity of peace that Christ loves. Very directly, we see into Christ, as he is, and as we shall see again a moment or two later. The root of our mind is absent of being Christ in actuality, so why not notice that our soul, our feelings, our thinking, being itself, is already empty, has been empty, and is filled by him, the angels, the Spirit?

There is no end to the here and now. We go here for a moment and find ourselves there. Christ arises like a sun. The earth is new and beautiful by a miracle. The world falls into the way of actual peace with glory and beauty surrounding him. Love is simple, safety is found for self and other, and the mother and father of birth are already waiting where we are.

The reason we say we are absent from Christ's love is because the perfection of him does involve continuous love from him in all ways. The meaning of this should be clear at a glance for other religions exist in which Christ's love is different. Christ meant to infinitely love all people, whereas one of his resolutions is to love all people no matter what they believe. The doctrine made the mistake of setting up many things in his name when actually they accidentally made the mistake of setting war, hatred, and problems in his name. Christ does not want another war, but in actuality for that, all we can do is learn to live in the here and now toward peace. So whichever aspect of Christ that is the absence, whether it is joy, love, desire, or simply seeing with the eyes, the best thing for Him is to go to actual peace in every known way. After that, the art of prayer is to look for new peace discoveries. In Christ's name, may it be done.

Self is not the only absence possible with Christ. There is the absence of joy, faith, all and each of the other elements of Christianity. The super agent of Christ is absolutely known, while the other elements such as absolutely faithful, absolutely virginal, and so on, are a different perfection. One might even suggest that there are other modalities that absence is applicable to the following pages such as "this" or "that," the "difference" and other qualities of Christ.

Beyond absence are other forces; these may include the cause of holiness, the cause of virginity, the cause of purity, the cause of saintliness, the cause of childbirth. The cause of absence is taken in the Virgin's name. The cause of prayer becomes the cause of the art of functionality. The art of peace, known as the art of simplicity, rests in the art of the soul. The cause of known is element known. The cause of loving Christ is thus. The cause of virginity is the cause of mind known, while the cause of mental virginity is the cause of none. The cause of resting in the known may be knowledge by a known. Too come to Christ via causes is the art of coming by other. The art of going to Christ by causes is the art of going by power.

To really purify a sin by causes requires up to ten years or the equivalent in repentance. Violence is negated in absence. Wars are stopped by the cause of peace. These are all known.

In absence is fullness. The opposite of absence is fullness. The absence of qualities other than desire is possible. One might try the absence of war, the absence of the good, the absence of power, and so on. Feeling is an important point; to be absent of the cause of emotional attachment is to fill oneself for the love God. Actually, the cause of perfectly negated sexual desire is the art of virginity. Negation is not the only alternative; one can double-negate, as well as to try increasing mindfulness of these arts.

The philosophy of absence, or emptiness, explains in part by Creation. We are created from clay. Clay, inanimate until God breathes life into us, may be empty of life. The sense of self is a negation of the absence of life. It is the same for other factors of human nature.

Emptiness, therefore, is the state of the person preceding in time God, the cause of life. So to return to that state of emptiness is to return to a natural phenomenon. The Garden of Good and Evil has many such states.

In the part of mind where the soul is not, there is spacelessness of soul. So there is no soul there; to fill such a space with the holy is not the main point here. The space where the soul exists now was once mere absence. Actually, the soul is either one or many. Because the soul is usually one and has similar characteristics in all people, it means that there are many similar souls. It is even possible to imagine all souls joined into one great world soul.

Whatever the case may be, the reason the soul may exist depends on absence. That is to say that for something to be there at all, it must exist in emptiness. So in this case, the emptiness is full of soul.

Absence of objects

Christ saw the absence of capacity in objects as their difference in nature from his love of humanity. Although we say that some of our friends are like talking to a brick wall, Christ does not believe human identity is the same. Therefore, for the result of human objects in Himself, for Him to know that absolute was also for Him to know that He Himself was human as though made of the mind of the world of matter. This really means that He "saw" Himself as a perfect part of the universe, and that truly speaking, He neither knew the world of matter nor did not know the world. In this sense, the world is the love of Christ. This does not mean that he had out-loved the world of man, but rather that He himself expressed the love in the world.

His love is universal, like the elements. The elements are not balanced to the same degree in each of us by human rights. He loved people, plants, animals, and things as well, such as food, the lambs, and his mother and father. So in actuality, we know that we are like him loving other people. Absence of things, in this case, means that they are not of the love nature in the absence of attainment in Christ Himself. So a phenomenon has absolute value in itself, as a Creation of God, while it has the significance accordingly by humanity. So God created all things for perfection, including garbage, good and evil, the problems of mortals, and so on up to the point that he identifies spirit as absence of himself within himself. God has a mind to do this, while at the same time, he is not too concerned that things are this way or that.

When objects are emptiness in Christianity, the world appears the same as a realm of the ownership of Christ. Christ owns this world. We may feel hurt by this, but it is what he can own with his bare hands and feet, his words are words he cans speak with his tongue, what he sees with his bare eyes, and so on. So what it means, that Christ may visit a major symbol of the world by emptiness, is that he may see it, recognize the complexity of God's Creation and walk away in the here and now himself, perhaps smiling about peace. The primary objects do not become by Christ, but he himself will not destroy them, because of the cross.

So emptiness is a part of Christianity. Christianity equals emptiness. Christianity is not just emptiness. Christianity is infinite like emptiness. Christian objects usually have a flavor too them. The flavor of Christ on emptiness does not fulfill the qualification of Christianity meaning to resolve suffering. Christianity may resolve suffering, but in its universal absence within people means that where two or more are gathered, there is not one. We usually think of the absence containing knowledge of another as the knowing of the other person; to fulfill love in another is to fulfill absence.

Emptiness is not the emptiness of something or someone, like a glass of water, or a dead person. The emptiness of Christianity is the capacity to be full of soul. The soul is peace. So no matter who we are or what we do in Christianity, peace, love, dishes, friend, betrayal, what not, we make peace between ourselves. The art of making peace between individuals for the world at large in Christianity involves many groups of people and many things. Emptiness is rather like a clear glass itself, or a bowl of light, the soul. The soul is made of Christ's love. We all have Christ's love, and Christ is the individual we see in others to benefit him by loving others. So none of us are really empty, but it is a natural phenomenon to be able to know another, to have love between people, and to know that emptiness, in part, makes it possible. So we choose peace in the world, globally, mentally, with our children, friends, and family so that His prayers may be answered for something actual, like a gift, to all people. Many ways of peace already exist, but there is only one actual peace, and that is peace from war in the world.

Does Christ complete emptiness? The answer is complex and difficult. Rather than empty himself through time, Christ empowers or least powers, as is his will, the known. He Himself found the way for us, but not quite as people of certainty ordinarily think of the way. It means that independence mutual is dependence nonmutual.

In the case that the reader begins to think that the list of phenomena under Christ's—a priest's—or someone's power, he or she should think carefully about

Jesus and his connection to heaven. How many items on a list could a mortal human like Christ actually supply in his lifetime? The answer is simple. He probably listed a few things out loud and had nothing less on his thinking than other quite-ordinary matters.

So one should not think that a more elaborate system of thought about what to learn is greater. As we all know the simple, or the simple simple is very positive in the world. In fact, to pray, it is best to fulfill was is in the back, or the deep, of the mind toward the longer positive in the future. Simply, one would open the deep mind of Christians to look for the truths of emptiness. Christ causing the known and the known of Christ is a mystery of causes of aspects of Christ and known. The all known is unknowable, and on this point, Christ did not know the future of mankind in detail; he knew the roots of the nature of people

The nature of the soul is continuous. It is continuous in a particular way of humanity. As previously noted, the soul is continuous as a spiritual connection of the body.

Absence of Internal Object-Element

The absence of internal objects in Christ actually means that the voidness in Himself of hatred is there because hatred is not possible for Him. In a more profound way, that Christ is the expression of human love, then we become human to show that we peace each other as Christ loves everyone. This sense of absence is not a negative of our own human nature. How much of Christ's love does the individual need? None. Christ had no hatred or war in Himself but, to the contrary, had great faith, which fulfilled into a love of all people, everywhere, at all times. So before Christ, the world was empty of love, and He found the absence and fills it in us. When we know His love, then His love is the positive absence, and when we suffer, suffering is the absence of His hatred. It is very vague in a way, and it requires careful practice by specific knowledge of peace to know about His internal objects. Christ's spiritual-mental internal objects are our spiritual mental objects. Each of us is different from Christ, while we are known for humanity, like him as well. When I say "I love my son," I may mean that I love Christ, but as well, I love the soul of the person I call my son. The emphasis here is on the person I call my son.

The sense of an internal "thing" does not mean something physical, yet what I am talking about closely connects to the body. I love my son and daughter because the soul is owned in their body and mind. Elements of the body, mind, soul, and life make up this the people on the earth. So a soul-body thing encompasses everything that makes up a person. Then the "thing" of an individual (the individual element) is exactly that which I believe in the here and now. To try to find out what is right and wrong may be possible, but in actuality, the right course for us is in the soul toward peace, and the world's ways should be followed accordingly. Each person has his or her own way, whether she is walking in the forest enjoying the sun and the pines, to working for NATO, to giving a sermon in a church, each of these activities is a specific, moment to moment activity of life. For some of us our way is life, or for all of us, our way is our own specific life path in the here and now of the world.

So internally, one of the elements is the soul. There are other elements, one of which is the person as a whole. Another is the individuality, the nature, the intelligence, the mind, the body, the parts of the body. Another element qualifies association. Subjectivity, likewise, manages element.

Do these exist? The answer is that they do. The answer is minimized by several factors. One of these is time. Over time, the soul will forget its catalogues, qualities, love, and dislikes. This means that there is a permanent soul but that it only contains its own permanency. Generally the mind is an object of the soul, whereas the soul cannot be object of intelligence, love, sanity, and so on. At this point is a conflict between the dominant factors of mind. The central point to keep in mind is the compassionate attitude of Christ.

How do we know the soul exists in relation to minds, intelligence, and others, when they must be in balance in the self? The question proposes that the soul must exist in relation to something. Because object nature is such and such, the self nature is so and so. Mind, intelligence, nature, soul—these are all different. They are different capacities of the mind and to eliminate one complete weakens the whole. In the meantime, one is not complete without the elements required of oneself. The question awakens a thought about equality; does the Anencephalic child equal the "healthy" one? Either way, the parents are with the child.

So the soul exists nominally as a permanent entity. Unlikable as it seems, the soul is physically transparent and in this way has no materiality of persons and things. It is not exactly an internal object, but rather a tendency in people.

The internal category of objects mean may be apprehended. These depend on emptiness and, in their dependence, are linked to the emptiness of God. God understands all things, including emptiness and its causes. He created the world thus. The internal objects of mortals may include phenomena such as impressions, thoughts, deeds, dreams and so on. They exist in something, while at the same time, if they exist, they do not have a range of existence that is different from existence in general. In this case, they either exist as soul, which we know they do not, or they subsist in the same way as emptiness. The meaning here is that soul attains the quality of emptiness while continuing to function in the hands of God.

Absence of Phenomena

Because we are made of this or that, like clay, we are phenomena, like internal soul phenomena. The difference element between absence and absence of soul are minimal. We have a soul, but the question "What is soul?" is irrelevant. This is so because the soul is made of spirit. There is not a "thing" that we can point to "out there" and say that it is our individual soul. The meaning of soul and the meaning of soullessness, do not imply evil in that a pattern. Soul is good, and soullessness is not evil. In other words, Jesus did not have a long time to think over soul in his lifetime, whereas mistakenly, again, interpreting the human as having soul only in a "in" the person, he actually thought of the human body as the world carrier of the soul. This means that wherever we go in the here and now, the world, our soul is connected to our body.

Given that Christ may think of all things as emptiness so that our souls may be there in the first place, and continue to be there, Christ is the one who does not see Himself the known as emptiness. He himself is not of emptiness, nor nonemptiness, yet he may be known for it. Christ, God, and the Spirit might say that all things are chosen by the emptiness, while not all that is known is emptiness. The point is not so much whether or not we are exactly fulfilling the will of Christ, although if possible, we should, but whether or not we make the choices of his intention for peace in the world. There are other intentions.

By other intentions, the meaning is of ordinary individuals, like Christ's own life for himself was ordinary. The question arises about what is there really in Christ at the end of the day, if we are all empty by Christ, internal and external objects are empty, and so on. The resolution is in the fact that the world appears the way it does for a reason. It means that because the world remains the same, the feeling we are left with is one of love and compassion. The primary object of this chapter's conclusion is to lead oneself to the point that they begin the actual practice of peace.

Knowing

The soul is knowing. With absence the soul is the one of all selves. Because the soul can imagine nothing, then the filled soul is full of humanity. The soul full of self is a selfish soul, while the soul filled with more self is filled to charity, purity, and faith. The soul knows the self, is empty, and the self is the knower of the body. The body filled with the empty soul is full of the love of Christ. Love, we have always known, is compassion, as compassion is actual peace. Sadly, because of our human capacity, we do not reach the perfection beyond perfection of God Himself. When love is great, and compassion is great, peace is great, while we have a limit fulfills in our lives.

There is virginity here too, as emptiness is virginity. It means that the Holy One, the Virgin Mary, did not find the world filled with Jesus until He was born. So the Virgin Mary had absence (not, of course, the absence of love, compassion, and peace) but rather, she was the perfect mother, of the Greatly Loving One. So the body may be emptiness, while the mind of emptiness is virginal, like Christ's mother, not Christ. So to believe in love is to believe in the possibility that love is a capacity of something. For love as a capacity is virginity, like the idea that love is in the mind, or the heart, or the soul. Physical love of absence in the art of Christian physicality is possible, but it is a different art.

Do we love Christ or the absence of Christ? It means that barely on the surface, we are not named Jesus Christ of Nazarene and are not born roughly two thousand years ago in Bethlehem. So to truly answer the question is to become absent ourselves and to allow the love that enters from Christ to enter into the silent peace absence in us.

Knowing shares in emptiness with the soul. Knowing categorizes as a deep state in the person. It is continuous (see below). Knowing classifies as empty because the mind may be said to be full of knowing.

The Name

There are various approaches to Christ's name. One of these it uses it to be filled with His love. Another is to hold on to the name, to cherish it, as through devotion. If we do not call, or cry out to Christ, what will happen? Although currently we will think we are like a Buddhist, a very different person, it will not always be so. If we hold on to Christ's name, He will be able to fill us with love by absence, merely, in person. The longer we hold on to Christ's love, the longer it will hold His truths of absence. In actuality, to cry out His name may actually be to cry upon the meaning He brings to life. So by keeping His name perfect, we engage the world to perform ordinary miracles of functionality with the capacity of Christ to act through absence on us toward perfection.

The primary perfection is toward a viable reality. When the prayer for compassion is answered or for something we want. We already have something waiting. What is waiting the already perfect love for Christ in the perfection of our ability to receive His love.

Receptivity is generally considered feminine, but there is a masculine variety. The masculine way of receptivity is often known by his engagement with externalized phenomena. Christ is a perfect example of the feminine-type male in Christianity. He spoke softly and gently of peace, love, and understanding between men and women. He let others self be His own leader and well faced the subject relating to others. The will of men is influenced by others, and Christ understood this. So His will was softened by others indicating that others' minds became the will of His own. He may have been sensitive to the world in such a way that he gathered the will, the love, the compassion into himself, not knowing He would be known in person for it. "Where two or three are gathered in My name" may mean too that there is receptivity in a group, even of all males. So it means that merely listening from the preceding moment of silence to emptiness, then another mortal's voice arises in person, and the receptivity is to hear it. You may be surprised that during a conversation, you will hear Him speak.

We may hold on to the name of Christ for like absence the receptivity to hear and listen to another is ordinarily Christian positive. One may not call His name otherwise, but also keep it close to his heart, even over the whole course of one's life. The Virgin, I think, will support this, and the name may help us there too. Many human qualities are in common with Christ, while their selection may take a larger group.

By not calling Christ's name, we remain in a continuous state of pleasing God. We may not call the name of some particular quality of Christ, such as compassion, knowing that his compassion will increase as a result.

The Christian Art of Contemplation

The first art of Christian contemplation begins with a prayer for peace. This may last as long as one wishes and can go on throughout the entire session or throughout the day. The next step is to remember the here and now. To look over the actual surroundings and consider one's state of mind should bring the freshness of spirit into the soul. The known of Christ comes to the mind. The person stops their thinking and either allows his purity to enter the body through the soul, or to manage to think clearly of Him. One could use the breath as a medium to perfect mindfulness of Him, as it is neutral, or else one might employ the technique of devotion by one-pointedness. This is probably already developed in some Christians by their repetitions. Then one thinks of a cross, the Virgin Mary, and archangel, or some particularly touching symbol.

Stop the mind for a moment until the feeling is rested. As the mind is opened by Christ; His trust opens into others around us. As though carried by the Spirit, the thoughts and sensations may radiate outward.[3] If one sits in prayer like this for a long time, the thinking will begin to stop a little more, and the awareness will begin to turn more toward Christ. It is natural and has happened for centuries with monks, abbots, and priests. What is really happening is that the mind stops thinking of himself and turns more and more toward the subject of the prayer. It could be Christ, Mary, an angel, or a son or daughter, wife, husband, or friend. It is best, however, not to dwell too much on friends, as the amplification that can happen could be harmful.

Meanwhile, the emptiness in the mind, through receptivity, is applying more and more to the surroundings. It is the readiness of the mind. To really understand Christ is to understand oneself. The elements of mind, body, soul, and environment can be brought together for contemplation. Within the major elemental groups,

---

[3]   For the Buddhist interpretation, see Pema Chodron's published works.

are the perfections of the minor groups. These are like the universe itself, the world, the continents, the islands, the buildings, and so on right down to the infinite space. If one is lucky enough, one may be virgin on these matters.

The virgin of the soul breath is one who may acknowledge that he or she is breathing. They need not noticed for true that their breaths are the breaths of those in the Garden of Eden. The contents of the body include the lung, and the breathing practice may be directed either toward bring the soul into the body, or to mindfulness and prayer. Contemplation is the essence with the breath. There are other virginites, for each angel, man, woman, and so on. So for each particular thing in the world, like science, there is a form of virginity in Christianity. At the same time, each thing's virginity may come into contact with the holy too. A pain virgin is very rare, but it might occur. A virgin to the known of all things, each thing, everything, and others may actually produce a very great saint.

One may use the breath as a medium to negate knowledge of good and evil. If we truly do not know it within, then we know it is impossible find knowledge of it in the breath. Purity too can be found on the breath, simply by resting the mind on the breath, purity remains the same, increases, or grows in power.

Contemplation needs something simple to continue. Actually, growing so acquainted with something, such as Christ's name, the breath, an angel, or the Virgin Mary brings the quality to mind. Always having these qualities or identities in mind changes and transforms the mind.

At this point, one might form for oneself a perfect kind of dream for remembering and knowing as aspect of Christianity. Mentioning Christ to the mind in a particular way can bring rapid progress. Without calling the name, imagine Christ with God above him, the mother, and the angel of mercy nearby. The circle of life upholds the dream toward a rapid change. Years of work can happen in a few moments with the right practice; when the mind becomes saturated with the light and love of Christ, the individual can go very far very fast.

The Meaning of Christ's Compassion

Christ's compassion means the most to us in the world. It is the perfection of the Virgin's birth. He loved people in such a way that all of us were filled by His love. Absence really means that we miss Him, but that a Virgin of missing Him not only misses Him, but remains in absence of Him or herself to know Him. We can continually remember compassion in ourselves and give it freely. To truly know Him, is, of course, very difficult, but the important point is that Christ does not make a mistake about actual peace. His love is great, but has been greatly misunderstood for a long time. Trying to understand too much in another individual at once such as purity, faith, hope, desire, love, remembrance, trust, equality, peace, friendship, and other is too much for us.

Absence may be filled with memory of Christ's love, here and in other places where people take up the memory. This is the community of practitioners. Memory, association, desire, love, these may all take a place in others by ourselves. Again, people have the capacity to remember, so when they are not, at some point, in their future they wake up after we pass our Christianity on to them, realizing that a small miracle of another known is known.

Christ's love is infinite and perfect, but we are not. He like the known of all knowns, and in this regard actual peace may be all we know. Another form of actual peace is mental peace. When we experience our minds by absence, we can go past this into the mystery and leave ourselves into the love felt for Christ to all people. Going into another in the mind helps us if we have virginity. Also, having perfection and sending that to another means that Christ is not the only perfection in the world. Ordinary mortal perfection enlivens the love of Christ. His power is to love and make peace.

In this regard, we do not want infinity or eternity. Too much in one place by ordinary mortals like ourselves actually bind to error. We know ourselves by Christ, but we ourselves are known. So the known of another is the same, or different, then at that time, we have His prayers for world peace in common. Not only this, but to have something in common is to find the root or our own compassion. We have the life of His Creation in common, the causes of his compassion, as well as all the world, in the here and now.

So the principle is there of an angel of self. In reality, this angel might tell us how to think our thoughts until they enter the mind of the other. These are all under Christ in person. Our dreams of others are about who they are, what is in their minds. The angel's name is Anor. It means who I think you are is by nature the same as my belief in God. When we think of God, He is as we know Him.

Christ's Love
   Absence of itself brings fulfillment of love.

Christ's Infinite Capacity for Actual Peace
   Functionalism

Before we are Christian, we are already Christ's known to Christ

Joy

Survival

The Here and Now

The Christian Art of Beauty

The Christian Art of Shaw

Peace
Joining toward religion
Friendship in person
Jesus and
Marriage to
Psychology
Objectivity
Subjectivity

The Christian Art of Morality

Book III

The Art of Christian Mystery

CHAPTER 8

Christianity is one of the prime keys to peace in the world. Further, it is the highest aim of the Western world. Alternatively, there is the genetic fault of the race. This means that the established norms of Christianity are not identical with the highest or organically level of other religions, beliefs, or sciences.

There is no meaning absolutely to any idea that one aspect of life is evil versus the good of Christ. For us ordinary people, life is a sense of perfection of difference. It means that in some capacity of our heritage, there is absolute value to our lives, like Christ's.

In this regard, it is well known that Christ considered Himself a simple carpenter; He expressed as all of us do, life. It happened that Christ uncovered the Absolute Truth, while we ourselves live a life of perfection on earth. Why is there a difference between our lives and the life of Christ? The answers are complex; one is that He was ordinary individual with a gift. Another answer is that He was chosen; in the same way, we are chosen for our lives, yet we will not turn out exactly like Him.

God, we are told, loves everyone. Therefore, you are loved as much as Christ is. It is not the same, yet, our lives have purpose. We might never know this; it could mean we appreciate something beautiful, or that we achieve money, or love between our children. It is specific to you, and I cannot know about that.

To hear a story, however, is a true art. It means that I would love to hear the tale of how Christ defeated evil. The meaning of the story is my specialty, and in order to understand the other stories of groups of people, particularly for the legends, myths, and histories of their people is the art of the same. The element of the same and the element of the difference compile religiously into the element of mind, truth, or soul. So for the lama of absolute emptiness, the tale is quite topsy-turvy, but also by the truth of the tale of His people, the truth that He is human.

To go into difficult mysteries is not the art of this book. A difficult mystery explains in religious language some problem, some art about the soul, angels, or the nature of God. To explain this as a mortal is almost possible, but it seems that Christ would not attain the language in his lifetime. The meaning of his life is not the meaning of my life, while the truth of Creation remains the same.

Just as there is only one Christ, and can be only one Christ, there can be only one you, one friend, one pet, one rock in such and such a place. Oppositely, by the same reality, there can be many arts of the known. One may begin to ask, how then is the human art of the known capable of the mystery of the divine, angelic, even earthlike art of the known? The answer is that it is the mystery.

So the mystery is the explanation of things human, divine, angelical, material. It is a problem of the mystery of finding your own way in a mystery. It is a life of living life's mystery. This repetition leads one to wonder. To wonder is to wonder on the mystery, and to discover the truth is enter the mystery of the truth. This is the closure of the art of Christian mystery in the individual.

Peace and Beyond

The next art of Christian mystery is that between two individuals. Who is the mystery of Christ when two souls face each other? Children probably think one mystery is better than the other is.

The mystery in me is somehow known to you. This may mean a great many things indeed. For instance, two people regard a panorama of a valley. One look toward the sky, while another looks over the surface of the earth. For the known of ourselves is somehow the others aspect known.

To elaborate conjecture that when I am known, the other understands through unknown. There are other states of the known human, such as the conflict, the uncertainty, and many others.

The elaborations of the truly known, in the form of the good, are often quite enticing. The facts of evil are also somehow known.

Known evil and known good is there, has always been there, was there, and will always be there. To reconcile these two is sometimes thought of as the highest aim of Christianity; it has been known that this battle is over.

Other aspects of life exist too. Again, one may compare pairs such as opposites, such as good and evil, similar such as good and very good, truth and truly, faith and the faithful, as well as interrelated matters. So no matter the philosophy or the aspects of religion, the world is still here. Therefore, the most perfect form of Christian mystery is the mystery of actual living. This involves knowing others, trusting, endeavoring toward peace, and the many, many positive situations that are yet to come.

Every day we pray or practice, peace gets younger. The strength of ripened peace minds, ideas, and souls appears to us in our dreams. There we are alive, happy, and free. To succeed even a little in bettering the peace helps everyone. Our courage to love increases; our happiness goes way up, and as we pass farther and farther, we find ourselves back at the thought of peace again. So we start over there and give out our peace to others. Christ is the way, and we are all angels of peace.

The mystery may be very simple. We may say "Peace," once out loud and think that it is something from our lives that we think may make peace. It may actually cause peace to say so. Similarly, mystery may function without our knowledge. On one hand, this is not misunderstanding. On the other, someone may think very differently of peace than I do. Subject to subject may look the same on paper, but in person, it is a mystery as to why two people think and say the things they do.

Mystery, furthermore, is easy to think of. All we need to do is think of something beautiful, or something we love to know that there is peace in the world. And why? It is because something beautiful we ourselves would like to stay with and look upon. To know God's love is to be reminded that we all want peace. The mystery here is that one who loves peace is greater than one who does not. We will want to stay in Christ's love and compassion to make peace.

A very obvious mystery consists in the thoughts in our minds. The thoughts in my mind appear one after the other. The reason for this is another thought. The thoughts go on, but I sometimes wonder who made thought. They appear to be connected to each other sometimes, when in actuality, there is no one to say that they are thoughts at all, that I am the thinker, or that Christ is not speaking through me. It is a sense of wonder.

Wondering why is the mystery. We think and then realize that we have "thought" the thought. Not much explanation exists. It means that there is no explaining the cause of thinking. We may identify something in particular, but the fact is we think, and that it is a mystery as why, even when we feel we know why. Our thoughts are peaceful. Why? Thoughts don't kill people, actions do.

CHAPTER 9

Worship

The next art of Christian mystery is that of practice or worship. The ideal is to conform to the methods of the church yet the better ideal is to gain one's own art. There are other perfect arts of worship, while the best way is to be like a little child. For him or her, the art of worship is to walk into the garden and wander amazed at the sights and sounds, the flowers, trees, ideas, to understand in other cases the arts of greatness, the way of the origin, the Creator, science, art, poetry, and the art of peace.

When a Christian prays, the aim is to show reverence or respect for God. The greater the devotion, the greater the prayer. At the same time, the sense of love should be there. The reality of practice is that one brings the grace of God to the earth and its people. So to pray is not only to pray for oneself but for others as well. It is immoral to pray for the harm of others, as has become known that wars are occasionally started in anger, hatred, fear, and are thus known as the Art of the devil. This is not just a curse, but also actually the human aspect of life manifesting back into the world from the world beyond because of our prayers.

There is an even more special art of prayer. That is to take the negativity of the leaders of religion and bring it to oneself. This is an art of compassion toward the human manifestations of religion. It is within the branch and a part of the branch of religion to help the people who lead. In this case, the leader is always misunderstood, because He was so full of love. So however we misunderstand Him, the art of Christian mysticism contains the ability to go beyond one's capacity to misunderstand Christ, while one's knowledge may not be complete of another aspect.

Another aspect of the art may be in the capacity not to leave the world completely behind. This means that one does not go to the extreme of worship out of respect for other individuals. It means that one should not take life. Particularly, as Christ gave His life to prevent such evils from happening, the mistake of killing in His name, or worse still, inducing others to kill in His name is a very great mistake, and it is currently the highest art in the world to reverse the mistake of killing.

There are layers within layers of prayer. I do not say so aloud, in all my prayers, but there may be an art form to the silence. For instance, I hear myself pray in particular words and thoughts, yet the one who hears them thinks quite differently. He may see the world in a way we do not understand, or he may understand it better.

The self is naturally already a prayer. Praying all our lives for the future of the world, just with a positive intention for the people and for the world achieves the aims of God. Christ is always with us, encouraging us in this regard. The mystery of prayer is the good.

In the meditative style of prayer, the action is practice to reduce evil in the world. We do this, of course, without knowledge. This does not mean "I don't know," it means we work with the good and evil of Christianity to slowly gain ground over evil. In this case, evil is positive or negative, positive and negative, and so on. Evil may even be the nature of the known, but there is a power that can reduce it in an emergency. So to reduce evil by prayer takes just a little of it, and at that time, a prayer transforms it into a known. The known, then, dissolves it into the garden and makes first peace, then some other positive.

The Mystery of God

Service

The art of service is perfect mystery. To try to help someone, to do something for someone is a special occasion. Going back into the roots of existence, why do we help others? The art is a mystery.

Going about our daily business, there is no explanation for why we wake up in the morning and the world is still there. The mystery is not about excitement, rather, it is about calm ordinary living.

To work in a soup kitchen or a homeless shelter, we feel love and gratitude. This stems from Christ, and nobody can say how. Giving someone a helping hand means something so deep to the recipient that we ourselves are changed because of it.

Charity
Faith
Love
Desire
Belief
Reality
Truth
Nature

BOOK IV

The Art of Christian Originality

INTRODUCTION

The definition of originality is this: that which, in the beginning, stems from the start, and which is associated with causes. Originality has to do with the nature of the place from which things begin. Originality is human word. The essence of originality is God, while it is unknown. For a human, then, life is life, and it may actually be an art of originality. To elucidate, that which is human is the existence of the human. Speech is the emanation of the self. No true sense of perfection of originality could be greater or lesser than any other sense although the basic requirements of humanity such as food, shelter, and clothing are a perfect art of originality.

Infinitely, to analyze the applicability of originality contextualizes all phenomena from the point of view of positive Christianity. Politically, there are reasons for limiting the human to realistic expectations for the Christian soul. That is to say that one may not change the world toward Christianity again and again. So the human mind, capacitive toward the Holy Trinity heaven above, denies understanding of true originality—God's Creation.

To relate an instance of the meaning of originality, one considers an example. The example should be Christ. The metaphor of a moment of His life represents the example of absolute compassion. The absolute meaning for Him is of the perfection of life. Historically, many movements, sects, churches, formulations, and others respond and act during these world events. Christianity directs all of its movements toward peace at this time in the world. Absolutely, the only aim is peace, while in the future, Christianity may have time for other aims as well. So the meaning of His life was for us today to love Christ by experiencing peace.

Grammatically, the words of Jesus filled the absence of His own presence in the world. He knew the others at that time did not know Him. So for people, the structure of a case of His love, that is, linguistically, the greater life of language is love, peace, compassion, and many positives. These are the ordinary meanings in the West of originality.

The greater meaning of originality in Christianity does not only come from the earthly self. There are instances that are known. One may examine the nun, the wife, the child, the prophet, and the roles Christians have fulfilled. Ultimately, the infinite survival of all people, each of us only possibly dying of old age, is already in effect. Further, the cross is many kinds of infinite protection, by the cross.

Perhaps other meanings exist. For instance, in the future, God's will may further be revealed. People of the future will have new forms and practices of perfection, new arts, and new ways of knowing Christ. Events may transpire to create books and forms different than this book is different from the first Bible.

Doctrine

There is a mistake in almost all Christian doctrine. Christ attained a greater love than anyone who has lived. The mistake of Christians over the last approximately two thousand years has been entirely human, and thus entirely original. I mean to imply that humans knowing the perfection of Christ, the Father, and the Holy Ghost cannot but help to fail dramatically. In this sense, after the Fall, we are truly obligated to make great and severe human forms of evil. The world has seen many mistakes of evil in its actuality, yet in the art of war, Christians' mistakes are the greatest in the world.

There are many causes or this; however, the important point is that war is the disease, and Christianity makes little space for peace. After World War II, the Christians made the same mistakes again. The art of aggression is too powerful in the Christians, and each Christian is obligated to find an infinite way to peace for eternity on earth, as well as directing all Christians' way to peace. An alternative is not acceptable, and speaking for himself, the author will withdraw all forms of aid to a noncompliant individual. There are other arts, and the reader who is peace positive may find that the more peace he or she earns, not only the more Christian he or she becomes, but the better able to release peace into the world he or she becomes. In short, peace increases the likelihood of avoiding harm, death, and negativity in all ways.

All along the course of time, since the advent of Christ, people have been forming views and ideas about all things Christian. Another of these has been that Christ is the inspiration for all things as well. This, of course, can range from the very highest positive to the very highest negative. I do not imply relativity, but rather, that individuals may differ with each other. The human nature, to the very great of Christianity, includes an equal share of evil unto itself. That is to say that some people of greatness do not fulfill against in evil. This should mean that evil is nonviolence against the winning over evil. For example, stopping a war is also stopping the production of another war because one has stopped the first war.

Doctrine is not meant to induce such and such. Doctrine in Christianity at this time in the world is only doctrine directed toward peace. The meaning of actuality should be clear in the reader. No harm may come from Christianity for its philosophy. So the art of Christianity is part and parcel toward peace, while at the same time the individual is obligated to find in him or herself the highest and most natural art of peace. Language itself, grammar, physics, and all of Creation can be an inspiration for peace in the world. In this sense, according to Christ, peace is His philosophy, his art and life, as well as each thought, word, and deed that God knows.

Only an animal among men knows of war in the garden of war and peace. It is the global art of remembering the Garden of Eden. Good Christians know how to live in the Garden of Eden, spending their prayers and their love for Christ on avoiding the beast in a particular way. It is only common sense to avoid the worse of two beasts. In this case, there is the beast of war, truly more evil, against the beast of good and evil. So when war is completely gone from the earth, there may be some return to the Garden of Eden again. Historically, this has happened several times, and the world has always been glad of it. I think back to the time when England stopped a war with Spain. The Spanish fleet was visible off the coast of England, but the Queen prevented their invasion without violence.

Individual Context

In short, the individual context is the lived actuality of the person. This means not of the world above, but rather than the spiritual life, the life in the world. Christ spoke of this a little when He mentioned the worldly life. We can suppose from analysis that He aged in his few years of life. So like Him, our lives have meaning to all perspectives, from the world above, below, and on earth. Therefore, there are limitless realities toward the individual. Of these, several are influences, parents, genetics, perception, education, farming knowledge, survival bias.

Apart from meaning, purpose, the soul, and the spiritual aims, it is known that there are earthly aims. These too are worth it and are not subsumed here in the idealizations of Christianity. This means that life is worth living simply, such as by farming, by finding that the world is enough, and God approves of this. It means that everything does not need to be so complex, so religious that the ancient, very ancient, arts of living are subsumed beneath it. Tolerance of religion also means internal tolerance. The important point here of the analogy to Christ's life is that He lived simply. He was not a politician or a complex artist, a mechanic. It is dangerous indeed to think of something beyond one's grasp, and in this sense, if the farmer loves farming, sitting by the fire in the evening with a partner and children, then that is the art of Christianity in its highest form; absolutely, he does not need to know that he loves Christ at all.

So the events and meanings, each phenomenon in the world, may be seen as an expression of Christ. There is also the greater world context. For instance, at this time, the world is turning at the root, in every, each, all, and down to the least creature, to the last atom, toward peace. Years ago, it was different; we could afford a ground war. Now that the last ground war has been fought, the very last ground war, then the world turns to a new form of negativity and evil, like the last time the garden was visited by world unification in the minds of all its people. It is my belief that Christ can cure the evil of war infinitely, but that He must do so in person with His bare hands, His bare feet, with His marriage, His footsteps, listening to the wind.

The trick, on a practical level, to making peace is to function in a few particular ways. The first is to live as Christ actually lived. He had very little. In modern terms, a slightly easier aim is to limit oneself very deeply from one's freedom. That is to say that the greatest gift is to give away one's freedom. This has many meanings, but one of them is to subtract one's own well-being, to limit one's actual freedom. For instance, if one has the freedom in one's personal life, the Christian practice is to give away truly, thus losing one's own right. If the reader has a lot of freedom now, it should be limited to the point that one loses one's own freedom, no matter how emotionally painful.

It is important to note, of course, that the full range of phenomena deserve attention. Once upon a time, philosophers thought a kind of light ray emanated from the eyes to make it possible to perceive things that are around us. Nowadays, we feel it is consciousness. We may as well feel that issues in this book are sludge emanating from the ground to think that I intuit knowledge of God! Christianity has come so far that it is suitable to feel that God is simpler, in our terms, than man, truly. This is not just true of animals, but plants, stones, oceans, the sky, and each as well.

There are then psychological factors within the individual. These may actually seem at a glance to be about the same in most people of one's own race. Actually, the variations between races are small. The meaning of them intraracially, however, directs one toward inner-soul analysis. As the soul learns of others in the lifetime, the less likely he or she is to know for true what another has learned of them. I have noticed in my own here and now, personally, that this is always the problem. That one tends to know oneself very well, while increasing awareness of difference continues to lead oneself.

So the internal aspect of the Christian's soul is the here and now. That is the secret to forming the world around one's own body. It is not possible at all to attain to the cause of the antithesis of peace by living simply. The nature of the Christian soul is very advanced in a very profound way, yet Christ is the way to peace. This must, therefore, be true of the internal minds of Christians. Many ways exist for people to exist internally, yet that self is at once in the mind of God and the mind of the person alone as well. I will not endeavor to catalog every instance of a human relation to the Divine, to the angelical, or to the devil and to the other angels of darkness. The art of lying in the here and now, where the soul is kept in the world, is not viable, and it is naturally the same as lying directly to God about the source of life. In a prayer to Christ, one might ask that the world will bring peace by love, among all people and religions, particularly in the name of the Father, and the Son, and the Holy Ghost.

People with training in psychology do not have a distinct advantage over others. This someone who will not break up with peace to make Christ's peace has not preserved Christ's life and other positives, but has also added the peace to Christ's peace.

So at some point in the future, beyond peace in the here and now is life. This means that the future is unknown while at the same time, we feel sure that known today is known tomorrow. For a time period, the here and now is peace. Perhaps in the future, the here and now will be Christ. Expletively, perhaps as the body of Christ is in the Holy Communion, perhaps we will find in some way the Communion in the Holy Creation.

The Holy Communion is now about bring real peace. Thoughts of war are a sin. The Communion brings us to the here and now. The true significance of the Communion has yet to be found for the here and now. Perhaps that is the best time to know Christ's love. He who loves peace above all things goes past Christ.

It is a mystery as to why Christ is always there wherever we turn. For instance, one might think that to aspire to something greater than Christ is a sin. Actually, when during such thinking, Christ's love grows stronger than our mistaken thought. This really depends on context. It means that I can leap in faith to the lesser or to the greater, but only than myself.

The mystery of context is the here and now. The sense that my dreams and my fantasies will be lost when I join Christ does not mean that Christ will disappear. There is something there, in the here and now, but what Christ chooses to reveal with the Father is something more wonderful than all else yet known. And why? The reason is that when the world unites for peace in the world, God ceases His anger with humanity. Again, Christ was mistaken by people in their context when they went to war in His name.

The here and now has the Glories of God. Simply stepping forward to become known for knowing where one lives, breaths, and thinks in the moment awakens something in Christ. We may call it being, love, compassion, any quality at all is possible here and now.

Christ's Life

Christ's life is the life of the absolute. He is called many things, but what Christ is in person is a different story. He is really the absolute sense; it was His attainment to the absolute highest perfection humanly possible. To the extent that one can conceive of such a man, to that extent is one also compassionately mistaken. His life represents this.

It is wrong and immoral to dissect Christ again. His life at that time was fragmented, broken. It is time to let Him live alone. As He was murdered by the people of His time, an act that we are still responsible for, I feel that He was murdered not because of His religion, but because of His absolute foreignness. This is not only racial, but religious also. As many people have guessed, some religions may carry a fear as deep as the racial fear of the truly unknown. That is, the Perfect One, Christ, gained to such a degree of compassion that people two thousand years later are in fear of His greatness. Other religions too have fear. It is important in this discussion to keep in mind that the body of Christ is not the holy body only. I think from His perspective, it was an ordinary body, thought of by thoughts of a man. On this point, one must examine carefully one's Christian body, to discern how he or she thinks of himself or herself, and analyze whether another's body has the soul in the same way, a different way, or whether the body of the Christian soul is known at all.

There are other points of Christ's life that one must consider for oneself to understand the true meaning of compassion. One volatile of these is the violence and religious abuse occurring over the last two thousand years. The problem of Christian followers' worship is the problem of the human individual. For us, there is some problem to gain truth in the name of the individual described in the preceding paragraphs. It is true that His love and compassion are enough for all. However, the problem of independence is rarely answered by choice. So in these terms, we should consider Christ's ordinariness, the experience He Himself was too absorbed in to communicate as the true basis for life. That is to say, one may begin to choose, only when one's one compassion develops. This is an attribute of Christ's life.

No one has ever known Christ as perfectly as He Himself. This implies the fact that Christ's transcendence cannot be surpassed by the human soul. The mortal generally has the perspective that the human soul is limited by the body. This need not be the case, any more than Christ felt Himself unlimited by it. The dreams of artists and thinkers have been inspired by Him, yet these people do not notice that idealization should not apply to another individual. That is to say that the attributes of Christ are His own personal affair, much as the author thinks about his books.

The Perfection of Peace

The perfection of peace herein is actually only a small fragment of the possible array of this infinite art. It should be expanded into each and every aspect of one's entire life. This chapter contains but a single key to life's eternity on earth by the infinite.

This is Christ's art. He saw past the earthly life, I think, mortally expecting everyone to complete the apparently simple art of functionality. For each of us today who has failed to understand a few simple points of actuality, the absolutely simple thing to do is to stop completely and go back to one's own source of peace. This is very simple, but also very difficult. These may actually be formidable barriers to the discovery of considering compassion and peace to be the essentials of life, rather than obedience, prayer, and all the well-known formulations toward Christianity.

The perfection of peace is prayer, which reads thus: "All people, animals, and things bring peace. I join them to Christ for actual peace. My thoughts bring peace. I can *not* bring peace. Christ, the angels, God, and all others join as I find actual peace in the world for myself and others. I stop wars with love and prayer; I stop wars with my family of humans. My tears are tears of peace. I can't *not* shed blood. I make peace in my dreams, as I sit, as I lie down, as I eat, as I walk, in all my activities, my life, soul, and heart go to peace." Here, to find a single atom for peace in the world brings heaven for a moment in the next life.

Positive Aspects

Positive aspects of Christianity are not only eternal, infinite, and perfect as well the here and now of the world is somehow the infinite and eternal. This aspect of the positive has a negative side that cannot be evil. Elsewhere the author intended that the devil is the negative. Actually, that speculation may be just about negative emotionality, if even by mental feeling. Christ may be the highest positive, consisting of the collection of qualities such as compassion, love, understanding, peace, and others, whereas for the man Christ, the here and now of Himself is all He had too.

Each of us may take our god-given qualities, and His love and compassion may bring thinking to ourselves, but the important point is not to dwell too much on the love of Christ the man. That is to say that our self, our person, should not take the love of Christ. This means that Christ the man, quite ordinarily, is known for giving while we too can give each other, very much in the name of each other in Creation. So it is all right to give to each other beyond Christ. This means that any positive is positive of Creation, whereas Christ the man does not separate from Christ the person, Christ the Child, or the Trinity in general.

Many signs and prophets are positive as well. Sometimes the racial difference is unknown in a way that makes problems among us. One positive practice for all of us is to take up the matter between people and work toward the positive gain. The perfection of this, I think, is known to us somehow. To look at another, such as a friend or a husband, mother, or father as though he or she is actually a person of difference is then to begin to solve problems among people. So for a Hawaiian, the art might be to think of an African by treating them like the perfection of Christ. Positive that thinking of individuals as your very own child is a perfect practice, indeed. For your child to be the prophet makes him different than actually thinking of him as having a positive nature. For phenomena as well, one should see ordinary phenomena as being equivalent by their creation. In other words, signs are not special and have no more significance the ordinary trees, rivers, and minerals. Therefore, when a sign is present, one respects it while when no sign is there, one appreciates it equivalently. And so, for each of the phenomenon in the Christian world past, present, or future, we form the peace view for the infinite future.

The most important point, I think, from Christ's perspective neither is God, nor the Spirit, nor Himself, but rather the person. For us, this means something about ourselves. We may try to express life as perfectly as we can, or we may simply try our hardest. If possible, one should try even more strongly toward another person than oneself. This means that if we are capable of thinking of another person at all, we should aim toward Christian responsibility, infinitely. An example may be as simple as giving another person the thought of peace for the very first time and always supporting them thus. Also, responsibility may be extended toward each individual, particularly through prayer.

The positive in general is life itself. Life is within religion, and religion is within life. God created life, and God created positive and negative truth. The Bible is positive insofar as it brings peace to the world and other positives, but it has become increasingly apparent that the positives and the negatives are difficult to identify permanently. Positively to decide does not agree with all others, yet the truth is known. The millions of Christians agree to go to peace by Christ. So the positive of religion are everywhere, the negative are everywhere too, though to avoid both leads elsewhere. One of these is to positive evil and one is to negative. Positive factuality explains permanently that war actually has no positive aspects. Similarly, factuality explains that war goes beyond negative evil into the form of the devil in person. He and his minions walk among us now and will walk among us forever.

Actually, the devil is a dream; because of our nature, we feel he is a human mortal. Reality realizes that the devil inhabits this world invisibly. He cannot be known to us, as he too is somehow not real. So Christ, the man, had a different nature, the opposite of evil. Yet because of His nature, He was not a thief who replaced evil in Himself with good. Rather, Christ was born to arise to the height He did. So perfectly, the devil has never been born. He does not live among us as the good spirit world does. The evil in the world is more than impermanent. The evil in the world is more than delusion. The evil in the world is more that illusion. The evil in the world has a different entity of existence than that of heaven. He is not a spirit. The answer to the question is peace.

Human Choice

To choose for a Christian has become genetic. There is no question of superiority or inferiority on this matter. The point of original choice began with

Jesus. The meaning that follows from this fact is that for someone who is willing to try to choose, various positives and negatives arise. The important meaning for us of choice has the human capacity for choice. More important than putting emphasis on choice or specific choices is known as the capacity for choice. I find it intriguing that philosophers, priests, and others have attained to the decisions to make God's truth known for describing Creation. It is generally impossible to take in the entire world infinitely with one's bare eyes, hands, and feet, and this should be a cause for peace. That is to say that war cannot be fought by an individual alone with his or her bare hands, and also to say that one in general can't really own anything in eternity due to the lifespan.

Specifically, choice in general is not good enough. Choice is but one word of the infinite Creation, and God is not likely to have created us to choose for the sake of choosing. I say this from the point of view of human limitation in the world. Therefore, the correct choice at all times in life is specifically made of many other human aspects. One of these is the life situation, of life from the point of view of the here and now. The soul categorizes along with mortal love. From the point of view of individuality, the choice for mortal love is greater on earth than the value of any negative effects in this world above choosing the most perfect world for each and every people. This applies to groups as well as individuals.

Choosing, life is best known as an art of the positive. Categorically, the positive may be a very high bracket of scientific religionism, whereas it is not known who the greater of the angel of the positive relates to God in person. From this one should conclude to make only positive choices, or to choose the lesser of two negatives. The absolute choice, necessarily, follows to be peace. This happens at all positive levels—globally, nationally, politically, in every religion, and in every place.

The individual level seems very different from the intraglobal human choices. For the individual, the choices should represent something for all other people first, in its various known and future knowing way, followed by the responsibility to himself or herself. This appears not to leave much for the individual in person, yet there is Christ's way, and He Himself is known for individuality. At this time, there are various techniques of scientific prayer, science, worship, but primarily, one does not direct oneself of Christ toward an aim that is still already known. So to work out the positive aim of peace is to be eternally fulfilled.

The individual, furthermore, may choose cats over mice or vice versa, friendship over romance, chocolate in the morning, and many other ordinary choices while fulfilling actual peace. Many aims of life, such as eating, sleeping, using the toilet, relating old stories, and remembering relatives are the actual stuff of life that makes Christianity worthwhile. There is global responsibility, local too, and all the things ordinarily we take for granted. The natural representative of the soul, heaven, Jesus, God, the Holy Spirit, and so on are all chosen in the here and now. Church is acceptable, whereas living a simple life that fulfills the world may actually be a higher perfection. Most of us do not live in the architectural building known as a church, whereas to see the love, peace, simply, like a child, in the here and now may actually be closer to Christ's name than repeating a thousand Hail Mary prayers.

One should keep in mind that things tend to change slowly. Christianity discovers truth over time. To think that because one loves Christ newly moment after moment supplies the world with the right answers or one's own desire may be a great mistake. Actually, rapid change is possible, but life around oneself tends to remain about the same. Of course, sometimes there are sudden storms, or painfully, a relative moves away, a friendship is refashioned, and one's wife catches cold, but the important point is to know that on the inside, Christ's way in the here and now is perfect, and that people have always felt sorrow, love, desire, thinking, worship, prayer, and many, many things that really didn't go unnoticed. So God's will is for us to join him in the place where our lives are Christian, and also in the place where war is ceased. I think the phrase "peace and the sweet thereafter" is actually a fragment of Christ's speech, although it is understood in various ways, often mistakenly. It means actual peace, and the world as it exists after eternal earth peace is always actually there; the second part is usually understood because it is difficult to have a double reality statement. Christ's statements about reality cannot be understood by the mortal mind, although He particularly understood them as a mortal human. So whether or not it is possible to understand everything God says, the important point is the make the right choice and to keep on making choice to find ourselves in the actuality of world peace. After that, the perfection of the world is . . .

We should always choose the positive. Choosing the positive may bring highly negative events into our lives, even evil. To choose difficulty over ease, negative over positive, suffering over pleasure, peace instead of war at all, acceptance and tolerance over hatred and fear—these always bring heaven to our door. In the future, the choice we make now becomes the choices along the way to fulfill. To have a desire against such a choice is not so bad. When life becomes difficult, or when the world is filled with evil, it is natural to try to escape it. Pain brings effort. This is true of many factors in the world, both negative and positive. Sometimes we will try to escape choices because of factors beyond our control. It is not just a test—our lives have true nature, and our mortal flaws are not really flaws. They are flaws ultimately, but in actuality, God made us with choice, not so He might test us, but so that our own lives might not be so fascinated with evil. Of course, we do not always choose this or that, but in actuality, we know our core is choice, while at the same time, choice employs desire and any other factor as well. So choose carefully the positive now, as one never knows for sure if one will withstand the positive and negative balance in the upcoming times.

Language and Prayer

Several important points of internal difference arise when one compares various aspects of Christian life. From this point of view, the question begins to form, "What is language, and what is prayer?" The simple and most obvious answer is that language is prayer, but that prayer is not language. There are those for whom exceptions can be made. This is expensive and time consuming. Christ is one of these people. His language was prayer, and in many ways, His prayers have taken the form of communication. Body language, emotionality, life itself, all things, may be considered communication, but there is a special difference with prayer. Prayer is commonly known as the act of loving God. So the true prayer is the expression of oneself.

More originally, language, or grammar, is there in many points of actuality. It means that where there is difference in point of origin, there is difference in equality. People know that there is difference in the human race, but not one of value or love by anyone. Then we are in a position to understand each other in the name of Christ with actual peace thereafter following new ways of life.

The important point of language in many ways until the world settles down after the various problems that have arisen within and without religion is to remember, know, and to feel the greatness of functionality. This means that before one goes on infinitely about Christ and the angels and the Spirit of God in the here and now, one should afford one's time and life toward the right and proper activities oneself and others. So for a father, for example, of children, the art of Christianity is really the art of raising children. Similarly, for the divorced mother, the art of living is the art of raising children with the father. This essentially means that, one, the art of life is really the life of the art of life in the here and now.

It sometimes helps people to learn their particular art in relation to their talents strengths, weaknesses, feelings, problems, each facet, to learn to live in problems, as well as the positives of life. From the philosophical point of view, problems are a part of the positive of life, but during them, they seem only positive insofar as we can solve them. Actually, a problem is peace, now, and like the forever of the future, the next problem to come one's own way may be the actuality of spreading hay seed in the spring, harvesting and baling at harvest time, tending the flock during the winter, and all the other arts that make up life.

Sometimes after just a little time living rightly according to Christianity, we think we have mastered the art of living. The truth is that we have not actually done the millions of things we think we have. Our life is very beguiling insofar as the way to finding out what one has done is actually stand up, begin going to the people, and to ask them in person in one's own shaky voice what has happened. There is no other way. That is why one experiences positive and negative in the here and now. It has to do with one's true and also one's religion, ascription to a religion, and really quite blindly, what the other one has. Actually, it prevents war at all nuclear, ground, mental, spiritual, angelical, and others to make peace in the here and now actually.

Language, therefore, is equal to prayer by nature. What this really means is that the art of spoken language is not just functional, but that functionality, science, methods, life itself are functionalities of fulfilling God. To know love is, then, to know language, and prayer is first of all a language of silence. Silence then returns to God and comes back by mystery to the spoken language. Too many prayers reveal too little actuality. Too many languages of love reveal too little mystery. To evaluate other factors such as hatred by prayer defies the art of Christ. To employ language to overcome the negative of religion also employs the arts of releasing pain, negativity, and desire.

The art of language, then, is functional, but function realizes truth in a particular way for the soul. When language defeats the problems of negativity in the mind, the soul ceases violence of a mental-spiritual order. So language can bring love to prayer, the positive, and to defy negative mind states. When the mind is happy and free, loving and full of peace, the ability to worship Christ and to pray becomes infinitely positive and full of compassion. The dreams of men are full of life and other men too, so to know of others is to be aware by our way of thought-language that they too can ascend past the troubles of this life to know peace on earth and joy among men.

Love and Marriage

The art of the original marriage is overwhelmingly lost. There are various forms of marriage on earth, but the important point to remember is that they are earthly marriages. They may be under heaven, but the world is primarily the place for earthly individuals. True love in a marriage is possible with the divine, but it is rare, indeed, and perhaps only Christ could attain to this. Otherwise, matrimony endeavors to fulfill the best of all possible worlds. So in this sense, a man and a woman may marry unto Christ, whereas, they are actually marrying each other.

From the feminist perspective, however, the marriage must have the capacity for equality, trust, and mutual perfection. It means that to marry in Christ's name is all right, but both individuals must find an equal in heaven of the feminine character.

For a couple's children, the marriage is also to them. This, of course, does not mean they are equal in the relationship (until they are much older). They are the child-presents of God to the couple, and should be treated accordingly. Their little selves are the most important to the parents.

There is the question of marriage by a priest. If love is taken between a man and a woman in Christ's name, the Virgin's name, then that is a marriage. It should really be only mental, but taking Christ's name brings a marriage for peace. The reason for this is apparent. Once marriage has been taken, the wedding ceremony is one made to marry for peace.

The ceremony may take many forms, depending on the minister, priest, or friend. In rare cases, the marriage may be consummated informally by the church. The Bible too was written in Christ's name. The holy books are ones not of evil, harm, and negativity. The actual ceremony is ordinary, but begins with words such as "We are gathered here together on this day, in the sight of God to marry these two people together in the holy matrimony of peace." The minister or priest will continue in this vein until the ring is placed on each person's finger. In this case, the ring is the mark of marriage for peace for the husband and wife in God's eyes for peace eternal on earth and for children of peace.

Spirituality

What is the difference between spirituality and religion? Spirituality is religion's way of saying that another form of worship justifies reality. So for a Christian, the One True God is the known, and spirituality is the perfection of God's other infinites. For instance, one might be 99 percent Christian and take a passing interest in other aspects of compassion. Compassion is really just compassion. When Christ loved people of difference, he did not cease loving them.

One meaning for spirituality is that in the event that one is not born to a particular religion, it is the stage of one's analysis of the various religions. An individual may work at something and end up in the right place at the right time. Another meaning for spirituality is the Christian's interest in other religions. For instance a priest may begin to study Sufism to understand another doctrine of love.

The effort of the spiritualist develops from beginning to end in its various methods. These methods include practice, study, reading, memorization, prayer, devotion, and many others. An important factor is to "pass" to an era's tendency of the negative. Spirituality often tests the individual. In actuality, the problems of the world sometimes gain great momentum. So for a priest who loses a husband or child, the life test then is based on actuality. Make note of the fact that on earth, the access point to heaven is often so confounded with earthly actuality. One mistake in Christianity has been the confounding of calamity and unearthly correlation. This almost always creates problems. Known techniques of avoiding this misdemeanor are often scarce but are highly possible in the here and now.

The newcomer to religion of spirituality often brings solutions to other problems like these.

In spirituality, free thinking aims toward the religion. Religion gains from spirituality. To give spirituality power appears to increase the likelihood of authentication; oppositely, for the main body of the religion to donate more freedom is more viable. These counterintuitive solutions often contain seeds for further development. One very simple technique is to compare one area of one's strengths with another area of one's life and to draw parallels. Many factors apply in the art of Christianity, ranging from drawings on the ground, to fishing, to comparing geometrical figures, to dolls and toys, and so on.

Entering a Church

The art of entering a church actualizes the human aspect of the soul, life, or the person in general. It is a very dignified affair to take one's position. It involves some planning, to get there, and to get back. More importantly, one's bearing, or effort, is directed toward the symbols of the church. Thus may involve the cross, while the primary symbol is within oneself. The soul is expressed in this life by the carriage thereof in the body. The more holy the church, the better applied are the arts of poverty and wealth. The situation is actually reversed from the definition, for the less he has, the closer in Spirit to Him he is.

The other church, the most holy one, is of nature. Architecturally, nature is unparalleled in beauty. Who can forget the oases of the world, or the peat bog of Ireland once one has seen it. One's life should be one's church.

The next church should be the body one lives here. This means that the soul rests firmly in the body, not as a higher power, but for the body to harbor the power of the soul. The soul and the body are not really separate on earth.

Another individual as well may be a church. To speak to another, to know or sense them, is to be aware of a mystery. For the Christian, the other is often not well known. One should think carefully about the nature or the elements that comprise another person and decide exactly who he or she is. A highly regarded technique is to regard the other as a child, but this regard should remove the trappings of what has been added to the perception or the knowledge of other individuals. Another person is really just like oneself, while at the same time, the great similarity is countered by the fact that the other has led a different life and chosen.

Relationally, the art of friendship may be patterned after the perfect friendships on earth, always keeping in mind that the friendship leads toward peace, compassion, and the other positives of life. Actually, in the here and now, the other is very much a mystery, and all people should be the subject of one's love. Here and now, to love thy neighbor as oneself means to give of oneself and then to know Christ, and one must decide how much one is willing to give. It is best to live with as little as possible, so that one may receive that which is to be given. Discriminations about one's own perceived happiness or compassion are not limited by absence, but rather, one might have the absence of Christ's love, only to further His positive.

So the art of worship includes one's love with or without the perception of Christ's ultimate perfection. This, of course, defines human love as being free, while at the same time, God created man to love, the make peace, like His Son.

The church may also be the mind. We are born with mind and born again with peace, love, and other positive qualities. The mind, however, does need to have these again. We might get them only once, twice, or three times. Once we really achieve a positive quality, we no longer need to think about it. This is how to pass on the positive to others, maybe even all others. So once love has taken root, it does not perish. Rather, it continues to grow. Of course, we may doubt along the way, but in reality, love never dies, nor does the thought of peace. To listen to the sound this: "Death is dying, while life lives."

Questions

Christianity employs the question. Why does a question not answer itself by Creation of God? A question of an ordinary nature usually has a meaning about functionality. For instance, "Where is the coffee?" Another form of question has to do with human nature. We may try to find out about another's emotion, such as anger, the person thinking, or some other matter.

If, however, I ask someone about the soul, I will need to find out more. Life determinants, life knowledge, and factors of the world are too complex to understand. So we know that the world is too complex to understand our own lives as well as someone else's. This assertion is true because of our human limit. I can only conceptualize so much, while the employment of logic shows that conceptuality too is not all that I know makes the other the known. The other is comprised of the known whereas oneself is known as well. So there is room for the same, while the difference is comprised of other factors such as life's infinite tendency.

The Christian wants to ask a holy question. The Christian's holy question is in the rhythm of life. Life has many answers. Infinite questions may be "life is peace," "life is positive," "life is difficult," and so on. In fact, life may be the answer to life. A question becomes a problem for us when the spiritual value of the answer outweighs the realities of life. To get our hooks, so to speak, into something we want and then to never let go, reminds of the wicked. To get something and never take it to ourselves at all is the art of a question.

A question appears to a child as something Mommy and Daddy can answer. To the adult too, God and the angels answer. We don't get to the answer to our own question. The reason for this is that we have asked, in the beginning of our question for the question, not the answer. He who asks the question gives the answer away to others.

This situation appears thus. I ask God to know what compassion is. That is his gift. Everyone else finds out what compassion is, then my question is answered by the mystery. The mystery of the question is the question, not the answer. When God tells me that the answer is love, I may begin to ask what love is. After that, the question falls away, and prayer may begin to be questions without answer for myself.

One problem that always seems to come up with a question is that we almost always feel it is not enough simply that the question is. We think, we speculate, we try, we reason, we even steal answers from others. A real question asks of itself no answer, no reason, no feeling, no thought. Questions serve as a source. The nature of a question is itself. There is nothing further to add to a question.

Virginity

Virginity is not so much a matter of religion than the here and now. The soul aspect is known in the here and now, as well as the mind, the self, subjectivity, living things, language, symbols, and all things too. One individual does not do all these things of virginity. Perfection and imperfection depend on many activities, physical and mental, that do not comply with knowledge now.

Where our life happens, there also is our virginity. To maintain it is to pray or to otherwise act. The virginity of the knowledge of good and evil, the virginity of one, difference, objects, minds, heart—all of these are sustained and reinforced by the art of Christian mystery. How is it, for instance, that a woman gains pregnancy while remaining a virgin?

The mystery of mind too comes from God. The labyrinthine attitudes and thoughts arise from the source. These do not apply to all knowns because the known is a virgin mystery. Non-use ability is the perfection of virgin territory. Purity can spring forth from nothing into the heart and mind. Halos appear in the air, though no force makes them there.

When one can cannot say virginity, the body and mind react unusually at first. A feeling happens and disappears. The self becomes God without our knowledge merely for us to know we can. A woman bears a child with no loss to herself. God can stop the time, reverse all events' guilt through his son while nothing appears to happen. Positive and negative can endure the world through time, while the mind does not know of them. Knowledge and intelligence work together in mystery.

Mystery then is to protect a virgin. To combine this with nonharming others is complex indeed. It is an art of functionality. To pray our best, to wish, and to sacrifice other valued items is worth it. And why? Because harm too is a sin. Harm is a sin, because it casts an evil curse upon ourselves and others. To be released from our mental wickedness is to get out of it and then to learn to have never had it.

What it means to have never had something when we have done so is a mystery. This is a miracle. A real sense exists that when we are forgiven and it is undone, we do or pray for something for people who disagree. To agree with this point is then to give back what we have been given unto someone with a different opinion. Love here is the key, for it opens all doors. Just to get what we want is not enough. To work for amendment actually heals the wound of difference.

The Art of Peace

The art of peace means that all things Christian, from the creation of the world, the life of Christ, the births of countless people, baptism, the prophets, the cross in Italia each and every thought, mind's activity, the soul, each phenomena, every attribute of being all go toward positive peace in the here and now. Peace is not only an angel of Christianity but exists in the world within the greater universe of human life. So in daily matters, from walking down the street to going to school to marching for freedom, equal rights, trusting a stranger, prayer, charity, love, and faith—all are currently directed toward the positive. The greater nature of Christ, in this regard, contextualizes in the equivocal nature of the world toward peace. So on this point, Christ has wept too much, has felt fear, and his descendants abhor violence. By their mortal figure, they too tremble enough ago now to learn to turn the other cheek toward peace. Christ might say, roughly, "If one should kill me, or begin a war, turn my other cheek, lose the next war by not fighting for peace." This kind of conjecture is really only analytical, but it means that one attains by all means to express the increase in each of us nonviolently, compliantly making amends, and to perfect peace not only in one's own life but in others' as well.

From the soul to the top of the universe, here and now, we hear him telling us how to live and love, and worship for peace, along with all of his children. The human life is really pulled by many forces. These include the Christian divinity and angelical, as well as other mortals, life itself, the material of the earth, the twelve elements, and each individual object from by size, to shape, to depth, and grammar, synontology, independence, government, and so on. This is not only from the point of view of many but from the singular, unique, uniquely diverse as a race, the sky elements, and all that shines under the sky dark, light.

An art of peace may involve many things in relation to the past. Historically, various elements such as death, evil, nighttime, hunger, and others have induced not peace alone. Therefore, to understand historicity objectively toward peace could not explain causes by the holy on earth or in heaven as having war. This implies the immorality of the human choice of war. The important point of such a great mistake is not so much punishment, but activity in the future. Cause-prayers may be cast to avert the world into peace. There are variations on the Commandment "Thou Shalt Not Kill" including that one may not incite a war. One begins to study the science of peace in the world, literature, and the other arts of learning.

This art of Christianity involves other new practices of prayer. It might take a lot of faith in Christ, courage to continue, and also basics like math, reading, writing. Beyond that, education may be redundant. So in middle grades, the art develops further, and information becomes the key. So in the higher school, one begins to specialize in a particular practice such as gerontology, advanced peace mathematics, linguistics, grammar, Latin, and so on. Of course, one must not attain higher than one's place, as leaving a trace of war by interpreting a book like *War and Peace* might actually be quite a problem. There are various other arts of Christianity in this regard, one of which is for the advanced placement soul, so to speak, to interpret the old Bible for pure peace.

If the object of war is the race, then the object of peace is the race well.

In this art of practice, one sees only peace in reality and dream. He tries to from peace through his speech, action, and thought. The mother and father, the friends, and family—all people begin to look different, likened as to making peace. The sky and clouds, rain, fields and plants, the oceans fish, and harvest all go to peace. Our outward-facing mind goes to God, and peace goes to our neighbor. The act of tolerating someone brings them enough sustenance to overcome the negativity of their lives. They drop the negative emotion in themselves and others. The answer to their prayers tells them how to begin, how to continue, and how to form new ideals of peace for the world.

Toward Nonviolent Penalization

Recent worldwide efforts have led the peace inducing groups to act in particular ways. One of these has been economical sanctioning, the withdrawal of aid, and the psychological peace substitute for war. In dealing with the problems of nonviolent control, the author is treading on thin ice. The reason for this is that it has been a long time with religion and war, as well as during living memory by evolution, at which time various acts of violence may or may not be known. It is also known that in this world, there will actually be something beyond world peace. This is to be the world of Christ by the actuality of a relationalism redefined by whole-peace by every human to live here.

Unfortunately, the current world situation is under this historically mistaken force. So there is, are, variegated evil in the world. This is not really only the evil of war; so other evils, such as minor crimes, do not fall under the spectrum of the art of peace. I could envision a world of peace in which the evil of war is transformed into other evils. This vision is vague, but it might include a trust in which the children of the world are entrusted to other societies and religions under peace during certain phases. It seems actually evil to suggest that children have been thought of nonparents as future possessions, containing a forbidden genetic gold. In other words, sons and daughters are not taken for what they will bring but for a much smaller reason, as suggested by the life of Christ. It used to be that brides and husbands were the cause of war, yet it is no longer acceptable.

By feminism, or parentalism, another important point comes up. How do parents and the society at large raise and educate children to learn to live in peace? This is not religion based on knowledge; rather, the art of parenting involves many things, including the larger group of the world, the neighborhood, the sisters and brothers, cousins, aunties, and uncles. In fact, it is not unimaginable by peace standards for the world to join globally toward raising positive children for peace.

The art of child too, like the art of feminism, leads the world to peace. Children make peace before they make war. Actually children never make war. Only an evil adult could do such a thing. So the historical forces of the child, their little angels, the parents, the life, and their breakfasts all lead to peace.

Among Christians, the violence is usually mental or internal. Outside, the violence is very great. We do so without our knowledge and internal violence is a sin. This is far and away the worst art of sin in the world. It has long been known that impure thoughts about the self and other included murderous intention, sexual desire, and many others. The art of nonviolence, however, means something more. This is the beginning of a journey in Christianity so long that knowing God is infinite, eternal, greater still, makes only for us to try a fragment of the arts of positive and negative of mind or soul.

Originality and Mystery

Human originality and mystery combine to form a whole. Either may be taken independently, but they are best when joined. Love is both original and mystery. The original love came from God to us in the here and now as a mystery. This mystery is the here and now of the Garden of Good and Evil. This is not the only case, however. Love might be original being, the face of the waters, the first moments of the earth, while the mystery is our lives here and now.

These two factors, originality and mystery, meet in the self. Life becomes the art of many factors of life. Love is a mystery too. Many factors can combine in these arts. All we need to do is look for the here and now or peace, and the outflow of Christianity may flow like a river through life.

Originality may seem greater than mystery, when in actuality, they are two sides of one coin. The original face of Christ may reflect great love. The important point is to go to the here and now and stay with Christ for peace in the world.

Originality may be a point of origin for us, toward the mystery. To form the way of these two specifies, the meeting of two powerful energies. The positive is the join.

The Art of Functionality

I will give an example. I wish for someone to feel emotional or mental pain because he has said, done, or thought something that I felt he should not have. The person then does feel pain. This usually happens without my experiencing the effects of my mental wishes, prayers, or other villainy.

BOOK V

Angelicals

Good and Evil

Balance

In Christ's name, may this book do no harm by prayer.

Good and evil gently strike a balance in the world. It has always been thus. Personally, Christ defeats much evil. Nonviolence and nonhatred are naturally existing forms of good. Evil can be nonviolent too. The Spirit in the world does not tell between good and evil. This means that language as an object is an inhabitation of Spirit. The facts speak for themselves.

The truth known is known as sources of life. Life, or the world of the garden, does not show a preference either. Our mind is capable of many things, like our body. Many people do different things from their variously known island sources of good and evil. Racially, it is known. With infinity is the human lifespan. The life human knows of infinite within life simple. The eye of Spirit sees purity by humanity and compassion. Silence of love is not a cure, badly.

Because known, of life, is not solely all known, the phenomenon of other knowing is not spoken of as the known. Christ's name is known while personally we do not relate to his body. The truth of his life is life of Christ known to self of Christ. Absence of Christ is not possible for one who prays to Him. He is among us while His Spirit dwells in our connection to Him. So where He is, His love is absolute to us by our lives of Christ in the garden. So to harbor absence is to knowingly accept Christ for others on the medium of the breath or the body. The art of banishing evil is merely the art of the ordinary. In these terms, the author indicates that humanity of compassion has naturality toward compassion and the good. In times of great stress or fear, that group will need support. May goodly compassion, goodly love, and originality be here now. The here and now goodly balance against darkness.

The cause of good is God. The cause of evil is Satan. The cause of good and evil is God as well. The cause of the Savior is beyond causation. Cause of the negation of evil is peace. The cause of the negation of rape is virginity. The cause of good power is attainment. The cause of Creation is the mind of God. The cause of knowledge is knowledge itself. The cause of a holy body is good.

There can be only one known evil, while difference divides the one into positive and negative. Good spent by all who care to try matches known evil by the power of Christ. Truth carries good, while lies of actuality a negatively or positive evil, not and. Winning a war with good and evil invites the source to return to the beginning of life's cleverness. The known is resting in the known nature while the good is the absolute known good. The self in this case is who we are, the people who are worth it, the people who care more about love and life than philosophy. Positive personal traits (see below) add to life more good in simplicity. Knowledge of good and evil after a small gain remain constant by the times. Peace is the high good remaining the same while love remains the same. Even so, it is not as one speaks of it; our lives change a little as we age, which was remaining the same. Intelligence evades the beast at all, while love grows a glimmer for us.

Pride and aversion to evil may beguile an answer from their combination into time, while the solutions to problems negated in the past question unchanging good and evil. The good is greater, but only in such and such measures. To shift good to good again absent cause mind none. The cause of the form of absent good remains the same in Christ's good and evil by the cause of the forms. Known none evil causes absence in others of primary development of first form of pure good male thus fulfillment of the Garden of Good and Evil. The wayfarer of knowledge of love and hate is therefore the duality of absence believed none as the same by pairing.

We usually think the good and evil is somehow getting better. We think, "We are making progress." Actually dualistic thinking does not mean solving a problem beyond duality. In other words, good and evil are known. Non-duality might phrase good and evil as "good evil better." This is linguistics (see below). In short, because good and evil are always paired in the Christian mind, rather than, say, good is such and evil is such, the nondualist phrases thus: "Good and evil are life." And why? The defeat of evil comes into life from heaven. The pairing of the two-sided coin is broken by the third quality that encompasses both. Life sustains good and evil by own being, while the battle is fought in the spirit world. The greater of the two is not the point but, rather, the resolution toward actual peace.

Good and evil meet and cross over each other. The here and the now is a safe harbor from these two. We must work on the problem of good and evil starting where we are at this moment. Good and evil are ideas, but they can be nonconceptual too.

A. Time

The human lifespan thinks that qualities change more or less over the lifetime. In very long times, evil does not change, whereas the good always looks like the better. Good, however, is not more known than darkness. Objects remain almost the same. The human mind attributes many qualities and facts to the world, whereas the world seems to remain the same. So good does not increase while evil does not increase. By constancy, the world should remain in an extreme state of chaos. By many qualities of race, the human sphere approaches to begin the question.

In time, good and evil seem permanent. However, when time stops or dissolves, good and evil change; in actuality, the only evils we need to concern ourselves with are evils of the human world. This is not the only world, but it is the same world we all live in by who we are. So who we are as the human race can change over time, but good and evil remain the same.

We may choose, over time, to try many things, but only after a very long time will good and evil be known more and more. The major families of the earth change a little at a time, and quite recently, travel made time quicker. So as the world resolves the war issue, time begins to change good and evil. All things change, while all things remain the same. New things appear to be changes, but new things remain the same.

Over time, the battle of good and evil turns toward peace. This is new, but war was new once too, and that time has passed. Good Christians have always tried to win this battle, and it takes world movements to defeat evil in the world. The result is hardly what we might have thought. So what happens to all that evil?

This is an interesting point. Evil really never dies or changes, but rather, it is more like the counterpoint to good that starts the questioning and problems, the wars and test of humankind. God too gets behind these things. As opposed to locking good and evil in our minds, God shows us Creation. In our time, we should hope to finish our life purpose with good and evil and leave a positive something behind for others.

Time is likened to an enclosure around good and evil. Time keeps good and evil limited. Infinite evil is possible conceptually, but in reality, it could not last in our lives longer than our lives. A concept qualifies as a dream. Dreams of evil ruling the world are but dreams.

The author wishes not to talk about children.

B. Space

Space is not so much emptiness as it is the absence of material. Space may be alive in a very different way than we imagine. Space is alive in the capacity to hold life. The universe can hold electrons, protons, neutrons, and so on. The space element is neither darkness nor good. In this sense, what exists as space is not known for carrying matter. So matter may exist in space, whereas mind does not carry conceptual space.

Actually, evil doesn't exist in a vacuum. Evil depends on good for its existence. The human race is the imbalance in the world on this matter. The human race is created with choice, and choice is good. With other factors remaining the same and in balance, it is the human race that causes the greater good. We cause it among ourselves, not realizing how evil regains a foothold. Actually, mistakes of this nature happen all the time; it is not possible to finalize this battle to our knowledge, when in actuality, when our lives are over, we ascend into heaven with our soul. Actually, knowledge of the infinite is quite impossible. We can take a fragment of something we know exists and will always exist, like human nature on earth, and call it infinite, but in reality, we only have our lifetime on earth. After that, time takes us to heaven.

It is as great a sin to kill evil as it is to kill at all. Killing has a higher status among humans as a sin than evil. This means that to attack evil invites it again. In other words, time stops us from living infinitely, while good and evil exist always. We want very much to try to fight, when actually, loving evil wins not toward good, but toward love. Love is good, but the fundamental basis of Christianity is that of good and evil. So in this regard, the truth is a winning against war, where war is factual and evil. So time identifies various realities toward peace.

C. The Cross

The cross shows no evil except for the scars to individuals. In particular, Christ's death upon it actually wounded the world in a very profound way. The Cross itself too was scarred. Wars, battles, and fights of all kinds bother the cross. Mental and spiritual wars of the internal world of humanity scar the cross as well. It is a prayer for peace toward the healing of the cross.

The cross is the restorative in generous forces of Italy. It means that the problems of the world are interlinked, and many of them via the cross alone. So to gain an advantage of love or self or peace or worth may actually be a bit on the dark side itself as well; for what one has to offer, offers the absence. For another prayer, one who wishes to try it cannot heal the cross; a gifted person might try this.

The cross is, of course, the highest holy symbol of the land. It blesses and removes evil while, at the same time, maintaining the life of the people. To harm such a source does not conceive of it. To be warned, the author means one specific cross in an actual location, not known to many others in reality at all. It is a life release to see it, a source of simplicity. One should know well that power does not qualify as the cross. The mystery of the cross continues to aid the world.

The cross is a kind of protection from good and evil, purity and impurity. The cross does not discriminate between these two. The cross lives. It cannot die, but the hands and minds of mortals think that a small wound to it is too powerful for all of us. In God's mind, the lifespan of a human is hardly a moment in his other eye. The cross supports us on earth forever, but there is no telling how or why. The protection afforded by the cross gains safety for a moment, but the power of evil also comes to us. So in reality, the protection Christianity is a little stronger than the evil. To strengthen it, one practices, and to find other arts at that time is also to find more protection. A church is an example of a place of protection. The Bible too.

The cross, furthermore, has a mind of its own. The symbolic value is only one of many ways that it is just a piece of stone. It also has thousands and millions of other forms of value. Symbolic value too is transcended into another manifold quality of the cross. It appears to be just a piece of stone, but in actuality, it is also real.

The significance to us now of the cross as a simple piece of rock is that it will accept our offering of peace. For the very long future, one may pray, hope, and desire that the future, although unknown, will always fulfill the positive, or come what may. We cannot know the future, but we should try to send the positive to there. There is some infinite guide to the future, who may be with us still, but one should not think that he is really known. For all we know, recent breakthroughs in reality time, such as its cessation, may have come to us from the future ago.

The cross is one symbol that makes these kinds of ideas and thoughts happen. Other symbols include peace symbols, and sometimes the symbols are joined by a powerful world movement. The cross might symbolize a world movement, but by Christ, we should only fulfill a world movement by world agreement. Interestingly, the cross too can disguise good as evil, but not for reasons we understand. In this sense then, the cross is always good, even if we think it is not.

D. Earth

The earth is a holy place. In a world with both good and evil, one must be acquainted with knowledge of both. Some people say that they don't know evil. Others that they know only good. A good truth may be one that makes us laugh. An evil truth makes us feel a warning. Fear exists in both worlds, and everything but good and evil is not good and evil. Each thing exists in a profound way. For a better thing, the good goes stronger. This is difficult, for an evil-er thing, the change in another place is toward the good. So where one thing is another thing is one thing, difference shows many. All things are in the world. Good and evil exist in the same places, but in different people. All places are different, while people change over time.

Earth is a solid place, where the ground keeps us on the ground. The natural environment sustains us. It is more than just sustenance. The ground itself is the connection the holy. The cross now rests on the ground, like many things, signaling that we are from here. We do not know if someone can walk around the whole world, but it hardly seems likely that someone might see the whole thing with their bare eyes. So what does it mean that the world is so much bigger than us? It could mean that there is too much to see, too much to learn about for any individual. Spiritually, friends can help here too.

The earth has been known to all people since they were alive. The original people, however, many there were at first, noticed the ground. Good and evil can't not appear in the ground. Only the minds of the people on the earth know good and evil and how not to know them.

The earth naturally supports the cross. It is an earth symbol, a worldwide symbol. There is a problem, and that is peace with other earth symbols. For instance, a tree is a real thing; to reconcile ourselves with Christ and God is to reconcile and make peace with all other symbols. Actually evil peace is possible by the earth; this is actually a desirable goal. As noted above, evil is constant in the world, but other forms of evil are there besides Satan. At this level, the earth requests original arts of freedom to release other islands to discover art.

Sameness, Difference of Good and Evil

Good and evil name the highest levels of Christianity. Other levels are there—for instance, the elemental levels.

Mind

What is mind? Good and evil are in the mind only. This means, rather, that the person who has the mind also has a mind for good and evil.

Belief

Belief is a primary means for good and evil to exist. Belief opens the door to the good only. Actually an evil worshipper can open the door to evil in many people. That is why a worshipper of war is known for evil. Belief in peace, or Christ, attains to the good. Whereas we imagine we can destroy all evil, the actual situation is that we can win out a little, and then finish that level of it over many years.

For instance, it required a significant time to learn and understand how the Virgin Mary bore Christ. This mystery explains something about the peace movement. At first, it was very hard to make others listen; now it is commonplace and grows stronger and more rational every day.

Love

Love is a power in the world. To apply love to the problem of good and evil means that human nature has the capacity beyond knowledge to love. To love, however, is not always paired with peace. Peace can easily be paired with war mentally, whereas peace is usually paired with love. The art of breaking evil, then, is to love good and evil without knowledge of either in direction of peace.

Hate

Hate is the opposite of love. Hate, we usually say, is a form of evil. Actually, nonviolent hate may be very useful. To be clear, however, hate can never be used to effect harm at all. I can think of many times in my life in which I had hateful peace. The evil of hatred in this case takes the consequence of evil positive peace through to evil negative peace. Hate, we know too, is antithetical to the love of Christ. He did not want us to hate. Actually, to hate all people is to turn to the devil. One contradiction here is that at the time of world peace, hating all people may actually be a form of peace. It is difficult to say why, yet hatred is one small fragment of all the negatives in the world. If there is a prayer at work in the world to control hatred, then that prayer directs the user to right employment of hatred. Actually, hatred does not mean that there is no love in our hearts at all; it might mean that our right ventricle is so full of love that the little bit of hatred in our aorta is a reminder that hatred is truly weaker.

Being

Being defines mentally and by soul as nonaction. Material being crudely general is existence. The person, in general, exists in relation to the nature of human nature in general, not material being.

A person either relates to good and evil as a part of himself or other, or to a material phenomena of good and evil. Being in this case includes a mystery of God, that of all people and all objects as potentially known all only to God.

Nonbeing

Death

Subjectivity

Objectivity

Compassion

Positive

Positive good and positive evil qualify in these three categories. Elementally, the positive has a high degree. All positives conform to good and evil. Yet there cannot be two that all conform to good and evil. That is to say that the intermittent changing beast can show positive evil of all type as well as each, every, and so on of evil. Evil is never good.

Positive evils include those known and those yet to be. The positive itself too can be divided as well. So for each positive evil, there is a positive good. The good positive might be said to be good dominant positive while the evil positive might be said to be evil dominant positive. Actually, pure evil positive is quite rare. Pure good positive is also quite rare. In the complex variety of positives, and combined with positive complex human nature, the absence of quality may fill subtle dislike of evil, even without one's knowledge.

Negative

Negative good and negative evil do not conform as easily to life as the positive varieties. Actually, negative good is not positive. Negative evil consists by such examples as war, murder, sin. Negative good consists in painfully beneficial, emotionally traumatic gain, peace filled with sin.

Negative good applies to negative evil. To result often unpleasantly affects the individual. One would be quite careful with a society-wide attempt for negative good and evil. To avert sin with a negative good, resulting in negative states increases the opinion. Again, it is equally wrong to go beyond an individual's capacity for negatives. Even in the case of negative evils, going to a degree of punishment fulfills the art of nonviolent correction.

Peace

Curses

This and That

The human is the person, or the "who" element in general. He is not a material element. Within the scope of many people is their grasp on objects of mind such as the thoughts "this person" or "this angel." Also, is the element called "that." These are not possible to know fully in the soul. The soul "has" this or that, while actually, possessions are material. Ideas may be purified, while they may also be tainted. To truly understand what difference is, for example, one must begin to understand it at all. That means that with the capacity of mind, therein, historically, the mind seems to have known difference, much as subjectivity is known. So between the major areas of mind such as difference, internal objects, perception, pain, loss, fame, and gain, there is a capacity for division (or unity) in the person. It means, for instance, that one might call difference this and sameness that. So which is it? good and evil.

Book VI

The Art of Christian Subjectivity

Mastery

To master something is usually to oppress it. For instance, objectivity has a very strong tendency to obliterate subjectivity. But first, meanings for subjectivity are made present. The meaning of Christian subjectivity is the self preceding the capacity for identity and the self preceding objectivity. Subjectivity preceded Christ in time, and it might be said that he preceded the movement of subjectivity.

Subjectivity also has the capacity for various perceptual objects. These internal and external objects are related via the core self. Subjectivity is also meaning, grammar, language, being, truth, as well as the nature of the person. So linguistically, the phrase "I am subjective" actually means "you are subjective." Pure subjectivity is older than most forms of thinking. So for someone to include in themselves, they are actually involved in their own perspective. However, subjective has the appreciation, in its various ways, of the world and others too.

Subject-object is usually a negative bias. This means that subjectivity does not know objectivity. So from a personal point of view, the subject is the only knower of the subject's subjectivity. The other, then, becomes the object-subject, and the human mind does not have much capacity to conceive beyond person, object, and internal object. So in this sense, the subject is actually becoming the subject. Racially, subjectivity is not known between races. Linguistically, again, subjectivity of one's own nature probably has religion; whereas variety is intraracial as well as racial-global. These comparisons, are not generally acceptable, except perhaps linguistically, or by the primary object of religion—peace.

There may be some interplay between time and space for subject. This implies that historically, at some point, the person(s) noted these two forms of existence. So the subject had the capacity to move toward new phenomena, if only physically. Time, however, may stop, and space may be perceived to disappear. So preceding this human evolution, we may now feel there is some sense of true absence of our past beliefs. Between present, past, and future, it is significantly difficult to form the present earth-moment. This becomes particularly true during a period of racism. It is firmly known that little is actually known by subjectivity, apart from the chance of one's life.

On the point of mastery, difficulties arise. The subject is none other than the subject. However, what is the Christian to think about someone infinitely great? The question points out that subjectivity is human, like objectivity, but rather than be crushed by the religion, it is best to think of a subject for the here and now. Objectivity tends to avoid the here and now realistically, whereas subjectivity is the one you are here and now. The meaning of known subject is known-not-known. In other words, subjectivity knows and does not know. So Christ's comment on the cross—"Forgive them, for they know not what they do"—entails that He had difficulty subjectively remembering during such greatness.

So is Christ the master? Answers have been proposed before. An important point to remember is that He was mortal, human, and subject. What He reached He got. Meanwhile, all the rest of us are God's children as well. Subjectively the tale of Darwin still rings true; so we are children of the earth. There is no evidence, in fact, that God is not the earth, but the fact that he can take any and all forms under the cross. That means that Christ can still become the world. This means any number or shape of things, but herein, it means that Christ actually doesn't know for sure what God is either, as God may or may not choose to know the world by what He is. One would not proclaim that God subjective at all, as He might as well be subjective than all people known, or objective than the universe. So the functionality guessing of objectivity is actually not known to us by Christ's subjectivity.

The answer to the question could be answered. The only mastery Christ realized in person was what He realized in person. This was really a racial matter. His ancestry is probably known on that island in the world. He is known there, I would argue, differently by the world's people. The meaning of this for is should be carefully defined aloud with a statement about what we really believe about Him in the here and now. He mastered love, but what do we feel to say our own innermost personal truth?

Difference of Subjectivity

In counterpoint to the last chapter, this chapter will not consider objectivity. Subjectivity is as much a mystery as the mystery in you. Difference is duality. Difference is imbalance. An illness in the Christian system creates a very great imbalance by the calamity of Christ's death on the cross. Duality in this context does not mean we sacrifice human life for him, but rather, that we preserve it. To protect and to uphold duality in the love of Christ is actually to maintain a very sacred bond of life. The purpose is, again, not to betray our human gift of the Creator but to subjugate ourselves to Christianity to any point of harm at all.

So the subjectivity has difference in the form of the survival of the species. That actually means that it is immoral to harm now or, in the future, any article of human life at all. This is, of course, a task for a great being, but in reality, the journey began at the time of bombings of Hiroshima and Nagasaki. The ensuing world disasters of mind, heart, disease, life, and death have now survived long enough to viably shape the human destiny. This is not a temporary matter of nuclear weapons but a direction to peace of war itself. The difference in life-subjectivity between war and peace is nil. It is therefore a one-way path taken up by all leaders for all eternity, and the infinite as well.

To interpret the previous Bible by objectivity is severely incorrect. The Bible stories, in relation to peace, were actually meant to be the end of war. It was a pity that the world betrayed the actual peace declaration of Christ, even today, when it is understood.

Furthermore, the difference between opposites and such may be liberated by Christ's love into the peace movement. Subjectivity is the freedom from obligation to the higher sense of earthly science. Unfortunately, objectivity highly dominates the soul, to such an extreme that compassion does not maintain in subjectivity. So a powerful difference can make a difference of the negative.

Positively, the difference of subjectivity is that we all wait in here, sometimes wondering why compassionate science might verify danger at all to life. The compassion of Christ by subjectivity survives to abolish the wars against compassion, love, understanding, trust.

Subjectivity and difference by subjectivity know reality fundamentally. The isolation of phenomena and their expression emplace the mind in a freedom. The quality of difference does not specify the generality of phenomena. Actually knowing, the knower and the known are seen one and the same by difference in subject.

Subjectivity and Similarity

It is easy, indeed, for the similar to like the similar. This I think is the primary racial mistake of Christianity. Christians often think that because others are Christians, then they are subjective in the same way. Actually, the thinking itself is the same, but as noted in the last chapter, the subjectivity may be different. Again, for subject, there is the person, the external objects, and the impulses within. Christ is probably known for the sameness of compassion, love, and understanding. Meanwhile, with sameness, there are/is no duality with Him. A known problem exists with all people being the same—that is that the object-impulse becomes confused in the person.

Subject toward peace on the matter of similarity is then known for subjectivity of division of the same. Springing out of the self is a new brand of love of Christ, newly in relation to him. Prayer is prayer of the whole person as he has been longer than the world was known, true, but not known for being longer than the life he lives.

Subject after intraworld peace completes remains the same. Know also that subjectivity changes a little over time, particularly interactionally. So people remain the same, Christ is eternally one, and so do the elements of the world.

With the subjectivity of subjectivity the same, subject sees the self. Subject of Christ sees Christ the same. Love the same brings subject knowledge of love. Subjectivity by same says subjective constancy. Constancy in effort toward Christianity the same subjectivity joins to peace. Subject peace is ready to worship and to love Christ for peace.

Subjectivity and Objectivity

Objectivity tends to dominate subjectivity. This means there is a pliancy in subjectivity that is broken, or transformed by objectivity into a pliancy of a one-track mind. Objectivity, we know, has the capacity to obliterate subjectivity in individuals, and there is an art to survival in the world of all thoughts, things, and people subjective. The art is to preserve things as they used to be, and objectivity has a slightly different approach. Both involve the person, but objectivity is subjectivity exclusive while subjectivity has difficulty reach into objectivity but does not exclude it.

So subjectivity is in the person, while subjectivity is under objectivity. It means that the person is called subjective, while objectivity changed the nature of the way the person is known. The person is generally thought of in some way as known to others, but objectivity as known in combination with subjectivity Subjectively known people are known people. The Christian goes back to subjectivity to be known, as one would personally go back to the land, so that the balance of Christianity subjectively balances with the objectively known world. Christianity subjectivity of knowing material, such as a bike in America, are actually not just perceptual. Christianity calls subject to a higher level—that of Spirit. The art of Christian subjectivity is the end of Christian objectivity. Subjectivity will produce less harm with technology and, at the same time, approach the organicals of life newly. The art of subjectivity is therefore deeply renowned for the art of originality.

Subjectivity and objectivity imply two souls each, or two selves. This can be resolved by the human capacity for nature must say. It means that the human mind is almost limited by human nature to formulate construction within the human universe. In this case, it means that the author can say something the author can say. From the preceding, infinite wordplay possible, and likewise infinite difference in soul maneuvering. The human race seems truly engaged with the problem of infinity, eternity, love, compassion, and God. So God made us a certain way—each of us human, with the various knowns, our lives, and our parents.

Subject and object tend toward primary good and evil. Dualism of subject object is not known. Knowledge of subjectivism equals quality of subject mind. Truth and subjectivity appear relative in objective field. Faith in subjectivity of Christ is a known positive for subjectivity induction. Trust in subjectivity effects toward judgment by subject.

Within and Subjectivity

Subjectivity is the one subjectivity. That is the subject says subject. Well enough. Subjectivity, then, seems a certain way to us. Does subjectivity have a within? Perhaps the reader should answer this question for himself first. That which subjectivity apprehends is the objective world, the world out there. But within objectivity, there is little subjectivity. Subject is subject for himself, as well as other internal phenomena. Perhaps perceived difference on the outside is not necessarily perceiving many on the inside. For the one subject, the subject is one world. To subject known subject.

It is not that far a reach to think of an individual whose subjectivity dominates the known. The technique is for subject not known subject himself. So what is left over in subject does not contain himself. So because the religious self is none, then the self of Christ must come through. Christ therefore reaches us within ourselves. The meaning of within of subjectivity in this regard informs source subject manifestation that it is there. The parts of the self work together to separate the identity of within. For the soul in the body, the subject makes within at the time subject chooses to call himself within. Because of the similarity of individuals and the differences, known or unknown, one gauges carefully all oneself to choose the "island" within.

Having bridged this gap, one becomes known for approval. At that point, the actual lifestyle within begins. The usual refuges are there—of prayer, hope, love, mercy, compassion.

We should make something of ourselves. The space within for life and Christ should not develop into some ordinary tool. There are many such tools in the past, and they will be there in another place. The art of living within specializes in life in a particular way. It is a new holy mind, as the soul once was. The permit is denied to deposit known evil positive or negative or known without world permission. One should think carefully about the art of not screwing up.

The subjectivity within is subject herself.

The Soul and Subjectivity

Angels and Subjectivity

Culture and Subjectivity

The Cross and Subjectivity

Non-Duality and Subjectivity
   Subjectivity identified with subjectivity.
   Non-duality means oneness or non-dividedness with someone. Subjectivity and non-duality at their best approach the true nature of subject. This means that one form of absolutely perfect non-duality has the identity of subject. That is to say that all subjectivity is somehow seen, known, or connected. So perfect identity is subjectivity non-duality. The best form of subjectivity is that of self-absence by perfect non-duality with Christ. Other perfect forms exist, such as getting lost in the mystery of non-duality with the Father.
   Each quality of the self known may be non-dual by subjectivity. To identify subjectively with oneself as Christ is an art. If one all identifies, then that is all identity. If one fragment, such as in the case of one's memory identifies that, that is that moment. Reasons for choosing such and such to identify with him subjectively are one's own business and should be found by oneself. A few examples include to identify Jesus with one's earthly father, to identify with him in marriage, and so on.

Subjectivity and Non-duality with Christ

Subjectivity and Non-duality with God
   The mortal mind we know cannot conceive but tries to think of the mind of God. Likewise, for many other facets of the mortal and God. Subjectivity, in particular, holds a powerful key to the mind of God. Subjectivity known subjectivity simple makes non-duality with God the art of simple living. Subjectivity cannot say that subject is more complex than God. Subjectivity simple is subjectivity simple. In this regard, any thought capacity of another being at all can be the nature of the subjectivity, of the subjective self, in relation to God makes God the known to subjectivity known. We cannot say known is not known, for the known is the known. Therefore, all things that pass before the subjective mind are known, while at the same time, known appears other than subjectivity. So in reality, the subject of knowledge is the knower of non-dualism with God.

Virginity
   The Virgin subjectivity is not just in the mind. It is the old art of virginity. The very core of the first person was ultimately virginal himself. In grasping how a mind could, in the first moment, making his way, is beyond the scope of this book. The perfection of this mind comes to us in varied forms. One should

know that the author's guess about the first of us is subjectivity. He would not "no" or "yes" a question of another for the question is answered by all of us. So each mind is the same, while we perceive the whole differently. The whole self is subjective, and then the objects appear like the known. For subject, the subject is the subject. It could be continuous, as well as the knower. The differences are self and other by age, preceding the problems of communication.

So the sense of truth of subjectivity knows subjectivity. The sense of purity of subjectivity is actually just subjectivity. For a deep understanding of subjectivity is not always one or the other of a pair. For not to take virginity from another in the subjectivity may actually be as simple as a little respect for one's life. Other activities of the world are there for virginity, a few of which are altering the mind, changing the mind, especially in Jesus's mind.

The art of virginity includes all the race in many ways. It is not just about the rebirth of Jesus, but of all people rightly everywhere. A perfect virgin bearing a child for all humanity is possible with many women. It is not the failure of the woman to bear Jesus but, rather, the fact that she knows the art as the known and that she preserves it in her own way.

All of life may be virginal, along with all of reality. Actually, one virgin left in the world is enough for all of us to make back in time. The art of a virgin bearing is known. This is a perfect art, an art of safety and an art of the known.

To find subjectivity in virginity is often to reject objectivity. The virgin subject attains by subject of other arts. These arts are changed back from objectivity by nature. This nature is subjective nature. The art of subjective virgin nature is known.

By finding your own virginity by subjectivity, one is really finding one's own way to exist subjectively. The art of subjectivity, of course, has perfect courses in virginity. One's own virginity, when found one's own way, may spell all phenomena by name for instance, by the list in the dictionary, superordinately by good and evil, by purity and impurity, by duality non-duality, ad infinitum.

The art of protecting virginity complexly adds to the problem. Protecting women and men often takes one to extremes. The sexual impulse is very strong and hard to manipulate downward; it is expensive, as one might say. By attainment, one cannot *can* protect virginity, first in one's children, then as children grow older in themselves, then in others, then in the society at large. The most perfect form of virginity is peace virginity, although one should be careful that one's form of protecting oneself does not absence fill with war. The absence of virginity can be known for the completion of another stage of virginity. The case is the same for purity, truth, love, compassion, and trust as well.

Subjective virginity untainted other's subjectivity. Subjective virginity is also untainted by other's beliefs. This is an art of originality. The art of mystery of subjectivity consists in capacity for subject not known.

A subjective reading of the Bible is positive for virginity.

Book VII

The Positive Person

I am writing a book about the positive person. This means something to me from the perspective of an individual with limitations. I have the same faults, the same sense of discomfort, each, and all of the rest as anybody else. As I was working on *Towards Positive Religions*, the question crossed my mind about who the positive person is, as opposed to what we believe, what is religion for us.

There is some overlap between these two forces, as one may say there is overlap among the lives, styles, and the knowledge of almost everyone now.

I should say something about my desire to extend a subject, such as the subject into other areas. In my thinking, I will generally explore a subject only insofar as the reader may need a lead to go into that subject fully. So if the subject of this book is that the person is such and such, I will only explore the topic of such and such into another subject so that the person may get my thesis to the extent they may understand in relation to that subject.

This book is about the meaning of the person. On a level that the only significance is the person. That is that if we are a young person, we tend to think in a certain way. So we see the world in a particular way, and if others think of us in a particular way based on what we like, that is their opinion. We might like things that others call evil, and we may like things that others call good. The truth is a different matter. So whoever we may be, there are people who have been known for the positive, and in this sense, their characters have been the greatest known.

In regard to religion, I will assume the reader is acquainted with the world's religions, at least in brief. In this day and age, there is no excuse for not having a basic, critical knowledge of the religions, but at least, it should be based on knowledge, experience, or word of mouth. So the reader should beware that in any particular category of knowledge, he or she should be sure that a shallow basis does not meet a shallow basis with the result that a book about the positive person is not understood as a book about something else.

So we have some way to understand other people. It may be difficult, in many ways, to try to understand someone, for instance, from the point of view of indifference, as though he or she were not committed to a particular point of view in relation to people. In this regard, one should really think carefully about what it means to be like other people or different from them in the capacity to be known. So many people have contributed to the knowledge in the author.

A further difficult point for many people may be that we are understood in some way by particular people. There is some way in reality for each of us, in which the only people whom we can say we really know are those we have met in our actual life. This means that in terms of the various influences on us, the only factors we really have to go on are the ones that we have actually encountered in the day-to-day sense. This may include the historical forces. For instance, the forces that influence me are not only intellectual at all; my father's family comes from a remote island in the North of Scotland. There are only about seventy people living there now.

So in another way, we may have heard, for instance in a classroom, of people such as the figures of philosophy, religion, science, and so on, who we feel we may have come to know of. So bridging the gap between who we know and who we have heard of, there is history. The meaning of this is that over time, we have met people who have met people in the past who have met people in their past who eventually, we know knew people such as Martin Luther King, Socrates, Genghis Kahn, or even their parents. This means that the knowledge we possess is in some way communicated to us through word or associated from the people themselves. If one searches carefully, one will find that the ideas that have died out are those ideas that did not reach the present through communication. They are not really dead, and one can find them in one's own life if one searches for them. It might actually be like the civilizations that have died out because of the nature of their governments, the tribes that disappear, or the forests and rivers that are slowly eaten away by our civilization.

As usual, I will make a brief note about the language I use. In a way, it is all speculative. In another way, it is all based on true stories of the past. How I know about these events may one day become readily apparent. That is a possibility. On the other hand, is an individual with limited life resources examining the things people have found valuable, true, or positive, and commenting in a similarly dualistic way about the events? I suppose one would wonder who the people were among the people of the past, how they lived, what they valued, and, most of all, what they said to each other. The ideas may seem elusive, but in reality, it is a language of many ideas focused rather loosely around a particular topic.

To any reader, I hope I have communicated in a way that gives enough information about particular styles of living so that they may reach into the next ideas having understood or seen in themselves the various desires of the individuals. For anyone who can read, then I might point out that generally, one really thinks there are things that makes oneself human. So in this sense, one might think that the things that make one human put everybody else in the same category. Although our opinions change, there is some sense that people really are people.

The correct way to follow this logic is that the corollaries of the individual, such as likes, dislikes, loves, hates, desires, passions, spirituality, and any quality one might name are also in another person in some way. So to the extant that one can relate human qualities to another, one should feel that what one believes about oneself may also be true in another person. So in this sense, someone who believes that so and so is negative or that so and so is positive might like to realize that the basic sense of the person identifies other truths about that person insofar as one is willing to grant the other person's sense of life in the greater perspective of the world.

There are some very general terms that one must know if one wants to get everything in this book. The first is the positive. I think the best way to define this term for oneself is in a way that encompasses everything one could ever imagine for the term in one's own life and the lives of others and proceed from there. The second is the negative. We often say that we are only positive, but in reality, we lose our car or a particular line of reasoning, and we say, "I would always be positive if this didn't happen." In the case where we are always positive, then that is our definition. In the event that we want to define the negative, however, we are presented with a problem. The negative is, generally, not something we want. So when the negative is there at all, we must know it and, realizing that it exists in relation to the positive, proceed in the direction we choose. A third term we might like to think about is the person; it should be clear that understanding the terms we use is not equivalent to defining them, but that in reality, we must know something about the person.

(further definitions . . .)

CHAPTER 1

How do we ask ourselves who is a person? We might know that we are people. We may ask ourselves about a religious leader such as Mary, Mother of Christ. We may ask ourselves about many of the particular religious leaders throughout history, or maybe them all. We might even like to say that the person who asks the question is the only one who can answer. In our own way, we should try to answer the question. We can say that we can answer the question, but we can only say finally that the answer comes at the time of death, when we cease to exist, when the soul passes into the next world. So the answer we give at this particular moment may be almost a sense of salvaging the person from the wreck the world has become.

Should we let a man live or die the life he has chosen? By asking the question, I am suggesting that there may actually be those who are known to know better. For a young man, for instance, may believe that he has a certain kind of knowledge. This knowledge may tell him about the world and its people.

This book is about the person. It is difficult, I know, for many people to understand the true life of another person. I know that in many religions, questions about identity or the question "Who am I?" are not questions that one answers in a brief discussion at that coffee shop, at the bar, or even, more often than not, with the priestess or wise man. This question of "Who am I?" is one of the questions that we must answer over the entire course of our lives. Of course, this may include some particular questions such as "Am I a monk or a lay person?" a particular practice, such as among the Hindus of the Atman, or even the abstinence of any other thought in the mind, but "Who Am I?"

So the positive person can be anyone, of any race, of any nationality, of any creed, personality, emotionality, and so on. Many perspectives exist on these matters. One of these is that there are many judgments of men and women for us to decide about them. They are not just famous; they may be renunciates, politicians, priests, children, parents. The real balance of all things is the positive, the negative, and the known. There are a few variations like neutral, partially known, unknown, and so on. In fact, all phenomena contribute to the existence of all other phenomena, including the positive person. This is certainly intraracial.

Personal Notes

There is extreme personal danger in making notes about the causes of beauty in the natural world. One of these dangers is in the human mind's capacity to believe that what it knows it can be the knower of causes. For a human individual to say that he or she caused the beauty of a natural object is a moral crime that may actually lead to his or her destruction.

Philosophy, as we know, may lead one to some critical kinds of places in thought. To recover from a sin of the intellect is not so much a matter of approaching a church and finding forgiveness. The real meaning of understanding lies in the cultural heritage of small groups of people. Particularly, as I am writing on the North American continent, the truth may only come to one through the blessing of the Native Americans. It was a very great tragedy, indeed, for these people when the Europeans came across the pond to visit.

A book about art is not really about Christianity. Art is not Christianity. A simple device, like a television, should really not be chosen as a representative for life. Most televisions are really quite small. I think the largest was about as wide as a horse race track. Apart from the enslavement of animals, the fact that a television has very little of actual nature in, on, or around it really means that one should look farther than television for life. It may actually constitute a moral or religious crime to write about this. One of the reasons is that the natural environment used to be quite different—not in the sense that the truth of atomics has changed but, rather that the inhabitants used to live very differently. It was a special occasion to watch a Roman circus. It might help to keep a plant near a television.

In my language, I think one can easily see that I personally do not have the capacity to describe the reality of heaven, earth, or hell with my words. It is merely a warning that among the seven families of religion, there has always been a terrible war. Logistically, we know we are all people, all equals, and all have rights. I could not begin to say how this world parallels the others. It is known, of course, that unholy language is a *sin*.

A personal note on Christ's family as friends:

It really means nothing to pertain identities to Christ. One should pray that he receives ordinary love from the people he likes. It is not that far a stretch to remember one's childhood and to think of how things used to be. One would not judge another by the "hair of his Chinny Chin Chin" racially either. It means that my other friends do not notice for true about another that they all recognized me internally. Or that he himself was at his best when he did not know the things adults know now.

> On the Liberation of Simon by the Hearing of the Friend
> He never lead a car horn
> School became fun this time
> An A on the way
> The girls don't cry.
> Love is good meal-chat.
> And Scott was a religious racist.

The Art of Christian Responsibility

Human Nature and Responsibility

Human nature must acquire more responsibility. Responsibility during the phases of life of difficulty easily gains great worth in the mind. At the same time, during our easy periods, others go through difficulty. Logically, by the good principle, the time to encourage responsibility gathers in the self at the time when there is little difficulty. An impression of the responsibility to peace exists for the mind that has known it. Everyone who is living has known peace; it is a natural mark of human nature. That we were cared for or survived is the life-mark of responsibility. It really means that life and the world protect.

Human nature stops at certain times in the world. Many people are stopped at Christ's door. The doorways to Christ are not yet all open, and perhaps in God's eyes, they open toward positive human factors. The problems of the human race are not just racial; they are religious as well. Our human nature has religion, and religion is known for both responsibilities. So as the mortal gains human nature, he also is given responsibility. The chalice of human nature is responsibility.

An explanation of human nature is possible. The various attempts to do so supply an art in themselves. Human nature may be an art, but it is an art of many. The reason human nature largely limits to responsibility by Christ assents to the responsibility toward good and evil. The mortal must never think of himself only in this life; keeping in mind that others are different so that he or she will not create great pitfalls for others, neither one nor many.

In simplistic terms, human nature is all things human and not specifically the contents of the moment to moment mind. To direct one's mental activities may be possible, but with a responsiblity principle or other scriptural notions, the guidance of Christians toward responsiblity by nature is possible. The mind nature is particularly potent for responsibility in its relation to decision-making nature. Complex potentiate more than simple, though not in the ordinary sense of the word. The complex cannot fail determined rightly, while simple does not fail. Beginning with will, the first choices of responsibility determine the later path. To maintain responsibility simply deepens the choice of humanity. Nature continues responsibility.

Human nature likes and dislikes, thinks this way and that. For the whole mind to go to responsibility, the individual begins with small improvements, then to the larger and larger. These include changes in the nature of one's life, the nature of one's prayer and worship, and, more importantly, the nature of the relationship to Christ as the friend. Other relationships with him are viable as well. For other relationships, such as with God Himself, he listens to the voice within of responsibility. This voice listens back; in silence, he may mean many things. To obey is possible, while to set out actively to make something happen by love or trust in the world brings something more to one's life. So we should act with responsiblity whether we like to do so or not.

Human nature itself acquires more holiness with responsibility. Holiness is the meaning of life. Someone who truly attains the nature of being in his nature truly acquires responsibility. Thus function of nature occurs over time. Although what actually happens often seems irrelevant or insignificant, it is actually the ripening of one's nature. Over many years, the individual set upon responsibility gains in measure the actual sense of being often mislabeled "truly holy." It is actually a practical sense in one's being of being truly in touch with things as they really are in the Divine eyes.

Holiness has the presence of perfection. For the priest who understands the meaning intensely of many true relationship of the beyond, that person has definitively done away with childish irresponsibility. As thoughts about material things drop away, the spiritual side of humanity shines forth, like a brilliant sun. This depends on responsibility. The most meaningful, the true, and the valiant of heart have done away with foolish things. For someone who can hear, it means that nothing worthwhile comes of negative ill-natured ideas and spirituality.

Human nature attains to nothing. In Christianity, this sounds heretical, but it really means that at the level of truth, where the soul knows itself, there is nothing beyond true worship. The sense of becoming a greater human, so common in our minds, applies in actuality to very little. So it is difficult, indeed, to be more human than human. This is generally true of most human qualities, whereas all that is conceivable is not great enough to measure or think of God at all.

This sense of human weakness does not apply to our day-to-day existence. Weakness does not measure in God's eyes. Actually, human weakness and the minds of humans only apply to humans in general. Only in rare cases can one see outside of the human sphere. The relation with Christ in such a case bears the marks of truth. So no matter how great we are, there can be only humanity among us. Our humanity reveals its most perfect side in responsibility.

Responsibility incites human nature to a degree of beneficence. To be full of love for others may be the will of Christ. It is His love we express, and through personal responsibility, the meaning of our love, or of our contribution to love, remains known by inspiration. Perhaps Christ is all of us, one of us, or whom the Father has chosen. How do we know Him but through our soul? The soul has the quality of the known attributes of Christ the man.

While noticing that we are there, are we noticing ourselves or Christ? The question is answered by our own absence of identity of Christ. So we are not nonexistent, yet Christ was a human like us. In this case, our own absence is the part of us that another person engages toward his responsiblity. This means that by our choices, small and large, in the here now of each of our actual lives, He

Himself is the ultimate guide, while we are like children with another child who seems to be rather bright.

So as we soften under Christ's spell, people begin to focus less on the *what* and more on the *who*. To know our self or soul with another person means to renew the interrelationship of many others along the way, past and present, and in the future too. The knowledge of the self is Christ, and He is the knowledge of the soul as well. The soul is not always the highest part of our life. In infinity, surely we might think of something other than soul . . .

Finding in our thinking a predilection for something that we offer to another instead of ourselves nurtures generosity. Adding to generosity or some positive trait applies further. Reasoning avails the soul a little life, while great respect flows from beneficial positive qualities. Someone who gives their time and attention acts from a sense of responsiblity. Among the responsibilities are giving, trusting, loving, enjoying, caring, remembering, respecting, worshipping, praying, and on and on. Logic too fails in place of love; to completely assert so however, might leave us as dummies. There is a place and time for each quality within us, including reasoning and intelligence.

Becoming responsible and therefore beneficent will begin a life-process in relation to Christ, God, and people strongly. By acting nicely towards others, for instance, there can be nothing left over to embitter others. These qualities bring great personal wealth, with no hope of gain for oneself.

Human nature in others adapts easily to the responsible. In aspect, responsibility fulfills the desires of people very well. To know another who is responsible can actually be quite a challenge. That person may not take things lightly, considering even a small fault to be of the utmost importance. Everyone will try their hardest for him, so that he might smile on them. A fragment of the love of Christ lives in all of us. So to be responsible about that seems like a good idea, but Christ does not really decide for us where, how, and with whom to show responsibility. It is a creative act of great religious joy. And yet other joys await.

The responsibility adept never fails. Christ on this matter let Himself die so that we might survive. He prevents war, He brings peace. To be at all like him is not to know Him. To show responsibility is to protect, to love, to ennoble. As mortals, His will is not always known to us, and perhaps, literally, cannot be known to us. So the choices we make are often wrong, indeed. To serve humanity and welcome knowledge of others shows greatness as well. Why do we not hear Christ when He says to love thy neighbor as thyself? The question remains unanswered because we are too ignorant to actually fulfill.

People like to adapt to Christ's love, compassion, and heart. In the same way, that which we love we tend to treat with responsibility. When we treat everyone with the love of Christ, we begin to know for sure that we are loved in return. Returning positives to people, even when we have not received, is a true art. Loving a responsible person requests responsiblity from within each other as well. People love the responsible because they embody positive qualities.

It is wise to become the responsible ones. The responsible are people like the president, the queen, the pope, and other leaders. These people are chosen not because of their great ability to manipulate millions of people; rather, these people perform because their character has the mark of the perfection of responsibility.

Responsibility is a subjective positive for oneself and others.

The Logic of Responsibility

Good and Evil and Responsibility

Irresponsibility is evil responsibility is good. This fits with the old archaic definition; the Garden of Good and Evil fell because of irresponsibility. Good and evil may apply, whereas positive and negative apply regardless. During positive evils and negative evils, irresponsibility fails everyone, God, and the angels. Irresponsibility ranks high on the list of known evils. These crimes do not warrant death, however, either singularly or with war. As the reader has guessed, war means it is the highest evil. When millions die in the Savior's name, why should we think the Man of Peace Himself would smile? He's actually still frowning about the wars of the past, and probably will be for eternity.

The guilt phenomenon in Christianity deserves a little attention on this matter. Not only the warriors, soldiers, pilots, and so on are guilty. The absence of stopping wars in the past merits the same guilt. I will not explain the sin of war in terms outside of the global relationships. War by assent or induction through other means gains the same meaning. So we are all guilty in the same way for the same crimes. Do you know why? Because the universal is possible. By human nature, there is a group difference in life energy, as well as that brought about by raciality, combinations of time and space, as well of course, as the nature of the religions deviating thereof. Individuals acquire differing levels of guilt as depends on their circumstance. Christ attains infinite universal true guilt so that others might begin to know life with less evil in it. Absolutely, the world of responsibility toward the good does not always defeat all evil.

Knowing our capacity for good and evil, as well as the failures of accidents, life, knowledge, and other factors, should make us aware that so many faults in our selves only increase irresponsibility. Faults such as ignorance, discrimination, incorrectness, unmindfulness, and others begin the chain of sin. This is an important point. Through ignorance, sin proceeds. Sin is not equal to evil by name; so sin is a characteristic of that which flows from the dark force.

Increasing evil and increasing good should equal the skill of those who can oppress war. Decreasing evil and decreasing good should equal likewise.

Combinations of measure of factors may not attain to infinity; our lives are finite, and we should deal with as a race only that which we are able to verily defeat.

To add problem to problem, consider that there may be positive increases and negative increases too. The nature of the known in this regard is to be of the utmost degree, wherein life maintains of survival. Generalizations aside, a known route to banishing a demon has an effect somewhere, and it is often not known in person. Therefore, the practice of prayer for resolution toward peace maintained by leaders brings safety and survival in the world. This is a very complex problem, and one need not point out that there are different religions in the world with a different human approach to the problem of responsibility for differently known good and evil. The problem is so complex and varied over time and generations that the right thing to do is to start with an individual one who knows very well; in fact, that person is right here and now reading these words. May he or she begin to deal with a singular instance of darkness in his or her own life once. To proceed from there . . .

Responsibility for all evils in the world is taken; even if only for a moment, one should assume that one's own actions, thoughts, and deeds have caused the evil in the world. A historical guide to the peace of good and evil is known. One can, for instance, employ all of human history in the form of the guide to cease a moment of evil in a very simple way. The person should not, as we know, try to attain to Christ, while fending off an instance of evil is quite possible for many individuals.

Responsibility, furthermore, shows a relational nature. This meaning here has functionality. In one's thinking and one's dream, one sees another in need of help and calls upon the power of Christ to bring aid to him or her from another in close proximity. The people in need of the most spiritual aid consist in those willing to go aid. Others include those in hospitals for peace, people in pain, and people in emotional pain. Evil actually lurks in the mind when no good is done.

Does absence or the nature of causality cure good and evil? Yes, it is possible. Other forms of causation yet not known may discover further methods. As noted elsewhere, the cause of the negative is the positive. The resulting nonparallelism to other philosophies is called known. At the same time, positive and negative themselves are known, therefore known Christianity is known. The absence of good is the negation of evil. Results vary, equaling love, compassion, truth . . .

The cause of good and evil known for difference, negation, positive, sameness, and so on attains in ordinary individuals to known. Christ in this case is known. God too is known. By the non-duality of most pairs in relation to the pair of good and evil, it is possible to negate it a little. This is particularly true of the art of virginity.

Responsibility can do no evil. Responsibility is not, however, untainted by evil. And why? Responsibility, a fact of God, grows like a seed in the ground of human nature. Because we are mortal, and because there can be only one Jesus, we know that we have the human flaw of good and evil. We have a limited point of view on this matter too, so we use the resources we have on a sure thing. Responsibility accepts the evil in the world along with the good, and ignores the nature of them both to go to the greater humanity. This does not mean we are given a license to evil but, rather, that responsibility achieves certainty with respect to world problems. Therefore, responsibility becomes the major effort of Christianity in the new millennium. This does not mean that upcoming peace attains responsibility for eternity; soon the wars will begin to fall down to peace. Rather, responsibility treats responsibility with responsibility.

Functionality and Responsibility

This is the most important point for human life; it actually means that what happens to us here, and what we do, determines our course through eternity, perhaps infinitely. To conform one's actions ideologically to responsibility positively encourages the art of Christianity. The art of functionality primes us and makes our lives possible. Our bodies, our dinners, our thoughts, and all of our actions depend on responsibility.

To become very specific inwardly about our actions is very important. One level of action is the physical. Another level is the mental. To make ourselves perfectly positive by action supports, upholds and makes love in Christianity. Responsibility fosters love, and it is a difficult art to maintain it.

Usually in our lives, the love of Christ takes an accepted, known form. Also, in ordinary, everyday life, all of thoughts, words, and deed gain merit or skill in action by practice, effort, and diligence. Responsibility, in this case, should take the form of lifelong mastery. That is to say that praying diligently for understanding for up to ten years may not be enough to understand one instance of associating. This is extreme; we each have talents, and some things come more easily than others. The art of difficult action, or thought, tests the individual to the highest degree.

These require patience, an art in itself, courage, valiance, and a positive intelligence. Not everyone who follows blindly should; not everyone of great leadership means to lead. The best way of all to master functionality lies in our attitude of humanity. Humanity should mean all the positive qualities of the human race or compassion.

It seems simple to take out the garbage. Actually, to take out the garbage during a difficult series of events in one's life may require something more. Life is almost always difficult. So if our prayers aren't working, it is some sign of mistake. So we make an effort in the here and now to find the mistake in our prayer. When it is correct, the positive of Christ will shine forth. At that time, not only his will, but the will of life and the best course for everyone of Christ, is chosen.

Furthermore, there may be some ritual of Christ, Mary, or an angel to performing some activity. For instance, every time one washes the dishes or prepares a meal, one could visualize Christ or Mary. The thoughts in the mind are actually under the control of the soul, life, divinity, or what not. These are accessible and a part of our lives. So to perform action carefully to preserve peace, compassion, or love one must act very carefully and mindfully.

Christ appears in our dreams. The reason is that we have performed some holy function. These kinds of internal relationships make for the perfect relationship to Christ or God. So in any case, the perfect way of the human mind is an ultimate, but there are other ultimates. The soul is one of these, and to live with ourselves and to know the soul profoundly affects action. Therefore, one must perfect action.

Ignorance and Responsibility

Ignorance is the opposite of responsibility. Ignorance leads to qualities like sloth, greed, and so on, right through to the nature of negativity itself. So the most true form of compassion is active, like responsibility. Ignorance takes the form of stupidity and removes the soul from the divine. For instance, one may not actually know of Christ the Savior.

Breaking down ignorance in ourselves is an art. Christ, for instance, as a mortal, never foresaw the events following His life per se. His words and deeds were profound in a particular way that has always had meaning and religious love in it. Ignorance not only blinds us from His love, also serves to obscure all or each and every aspect of Christianity. All of us can be mistaken, and all of us can find Christ's love a little at a time, when we are right about the truth.

Ignorance in the Garden of Good and Evil of responsibility leads down the path to darkness. The light of life shines onto knowledge to affirm that life is the garden, while mortals fail the tests of the Lord. Complete failure brings complete peace. To maintain one point is human; that point among Christians is usually choice. So by choice, if we must fail, we must fail toward peace.

It is difficult, indeed, not to be human. Human nature maintains, upholds human nature. It means that a human is born a human and remains a human forever. The natural birthright of human beings is their humanity. Ignorance could say otherwise. Actually, ignorance is the art of responsibility. Just as Christ is the art of Christ, the art of Christ is the art of ignorance. So holding Christ's name is holding responsibility. Christ's name is choice in a particular way. To choose once and forget and choose again at that time, actually means that we are choosing again our capacity for choice itself. When we are asked a double-edged question, to choose again is to choose the right path of Christ. This is always positive, whereas to take as much negative to ourselves truly chooses to break to choice again. So we acquire negativity to overcome and choose rightly, newly, the art of Christ.

Responsibility and ignorance do not go together. They are like darkness and lightness; on the one hand, a mind tries more and more to shade truth and love, beauty and trust behind lies, disease, death, and war, while on the other hand is mind of perfection, which seizes control of problems against evil to bring the world to peace, Christ's love, and the understanding that makes compassion possible. Ignorance is the dark shade, responsibility the light. Ignorance motivates actions like rape, murder, and sins of all kinds. These sins are chosen by ignorance in the form of an untrained mind, the mind of the blind leading the blind. Ignorance is blindness to faith; ignorance chooses ill over good, against even common sense and the laws of the land. Responsibility takes the truth, the path of least harm, the path of least damage, the path of least pain, the path of least gain for oneself with most gain for others. To find oneself praying for responsibility in pain deserves the space reserved for him or her in heaven.

With even one positive seed in the mind, responsibility can not win out with even a few prayers. The positive is sent along on a prayer line from Jesus to us so that we can not fulfill an actual responsibility toward peace, the positive itself, or to live him.

Ignorance means that the person proceeds down wrong paths. Oppression is a key example of ignorance. Not knowing how others feel when they are in pain identifies the negation of compassion. The important point is to take charge of ignorance and command it to leave the mind, like a demon.

Humor and Responsibility

Humor is a very powerful force, which never seems to really go negatively. Humor strengthens the human side of life, releasing us from the serious, dolorous aspects of responsibility. To tell a joke often takes the sadness out of a problem such as a serious disease like cancer. Wars begin by serious problems, and sometimes the hatred or enmity of long ago remains unbroken. Humor serves well to wake us up from the major disease of the negatives toward peace.

Humor is not the alleviation of some particular tendency. Humor is noteworthy in itself. Definitively positive, humor can break up the darkest of moods. There's a chance that in some way humor outsmarts evil. Of course, we should not be laughing about a nuclear weapon, whereas when all else fails, humor has merit.

If we tell someone who is irresponsible a joke, the effect can be negative or positive. In the negative example, the irresponsible person continues their irresponsibility. In the positive example, humor breaks the tendency of the mind to stupidity and brings a new fresh attitude to him or her.

Humor applied to the responsible tends toward the rewarding. In this case too, humor is negative or positive. In the negative example, humor detracts from the responsibility. In the positive example, humor strengthens and awakens the responsibility.

Humor, actual humor, is told at the expense of someone who is irresponsible. It means that to break the evil in the world, we cannot only become serious about it. There must be joy in evil, but there must be joyful good. The truth is that those who have eyes see good and evil clearly, laughing all the way, but those who do not have eyes do not see good and evil. There is hardly a way to tell about which is which. So the responsibility is ours to go back to good and evil and find actual peace. To laugh truly means that we are stronger than evil. God made man and woman good, and a good joke makes us know why.

Harm and Responsibility

Responsibility brings no harm to others at all. Through words, deed, thoughts, and the here and now, responsibilty cannot bring harms to us. The caution and care we use by our prayers works toward nonviolence. To harm someone is not accidental; our prayers via responsibility cannot cause harm by the power of Christ's love.

Harm does not apply in any case whatsoever. We are not, however, perfect. To really apply the art of responsibility is to become kind, gentle, and careful toward others in the here and now. To carefully generate positive prayers for ourselves and others, responsibility should take into account the fragility of human life. Everything can go from simple and good to complex and difficult in a few moments. We are driving on the highway, and the kids start to scream for several hours. The attitude we take assumes that we will not bring physical harm or negative mental effects at all. These are really unnecessary, however, to actually bring to others the opposite, pleasant, loving, good effects should really be what we aim for.

Complex matters such as conflicting religions and so on should be ignored on this point, or the religion will become known for negative physical and mental violence. Christianity is a religion of peace, and our prayers bring this effect in spite of the difficulty. The trick is to bite the bullet.

Harm mainly applies to internal phenomena. If we are hurt, it means that we have made some mistake in our thinking. Taking the responsibility, saying to ourselves, "Look what I have done to myself" is the key. Who else could have done so? The least we can say is that we will try to accept it. Christ always tests us, but the first test is to fail toward peace. If we fail a test, such as that of a major sin, then we fail that sin directly into the awaiting peace. This is another art of functionality.

Harm, specifically, requires of us faith. To have faith does not mean to think that everything will be all right. Everything, by responsibility, is solved already by the community of Christians within themselves. What it really means to have faith is to be willing to break our faith and move on to peace instead. So when our faith breaks, we fall into the art of functionality, wake up in the here and now, only find ourselves staying with ideas, thoughts, and prayers for peace.

Harming others is out of the question. The art of nonviolenece should have no question about physical harm. The art of nonviolence is really about mental evils. Christ's name in this regard protects us to good and evil. Where there is good and evil, there is no harm. To escape at all to peace is to know anything about Christianity. This means that the name of the religion of Christianity is in Christ's name. He was a man of peace, and it was good; so Christ's name is protection from war, and the community of Christians works together to pronounce the full infinity of His name.

Other deeper arts of harm exist. One of these is to take the harm directed towards others, like our wife or child or husband. It is like taking a disease from someone we know is too weak to take it themselves. I remember WWII and the nuclear weapons. Japan took these weapons to themselves to express the art of peace. The reason is unknown, yet it is unfortunate that we and our people did not take it to ourselves instead. In this sense, the Japanese are guilty of curing all that suffering. Christ's name can bring whatever we choose, but we can not choose peace, and we can't choose war. And why? Because the only nuclear weapons that will ever be fired were nuclear weapons fired for the first two times. It is impossible to actualize the weapons again.

Harm does not come into the scope of responsibility. Responsibility brings the opposite of harm; responsibility brings trust, human warmth, compassion, and the good. Responsibility stops harm, because we may take that mental harm going to another in the world into ourselves. We can redirect the harm by claiming that the harm was caused by us, that we have chosen to accept the sin and the responsibility. This is not the ordinary case in which miracle grants us power. This is ordinary. For instance, the author has known people who suffer from depression. At that time, he seemed to wrestle with the depression and take the actual emotion and go through it for the depressed. It is painful, but this is our responsibility.

Actually it is a mortal sin not to get in harm's way to help another. I think of soldiers who defend peace with their body or mind, or people fighting to save the environment. They give of themselves so that others may continue to live. The absence of suffering in a person's life means that they are ready to suffer and withdraw the pain of others. That is why we are all guilty. This may be called life sin or original in, because we know we are lucky to be alive at all; while we suffer, we want nothing more than to have that suffering relieved. Meanwhile, when we feel all right, we sin by forgetting that we can help. I cannot stress enough the importance of maintaining one's positive in the face of experiencing other's negatives. One should not go beyond one's capacity to think and feel at all. Actually, abusers are out there who will take advantage of someone who is willing to experience negativity. So if times get difficult, all we have to do is call upon the power of Christ, God, or an angel, and the suffering will begin to be switched off. Again, one should not go through too much, especially if one has other things one needs the time and energy for. For instance if we have to think, pray, hope, cherish, raise children, and do many other things, we should only try taking on a little negativity, pain, ignorance, or suffering.

Harm doubles the evil in a situation. On the one hand is the sin of harming. This is the direct result of harm. On the other is the absence of the lack of harm. This means that by doing harm, not only does one incur the sin of harming, but one also incurs the sin of not causing its absence.

On a larger scale, harming the society at large, by, for instance, starting a movement in the world toward the negative, registers in the eye of God. Doing something wrong, on purpose, to fulfill an aim that one already knows brings harm needs no mention.

Similarly it is a very great sin to harm the religion. This is not to say, of course, that one only benefits Christianity. Actually, the best Christians are the ones who do the most for all people. To help an evil man in pain, for instance, and then to show compassion to him or her, is actually so positive that the reward comes now and in heaven.

Murder

The sin of murder is an extreme act of irresponsibility. In this case, we may have forgotten that thou shall not kill.

War and Peace

War is irresponsible and, therefore, evil, while peace is an art of responsibility in itself. The bliss that comes from a time of peace is hardly worth breaking the invisible barrier into war. In actuality, the demarcations of international treaties, trusts, and so on are not visible like the external world. The invisible barrier is only in our minds. Like fear, we cannot see it. While we wonder what it is that will stop the war, we don't actually know what could stop a war. So the line coming back from a war is actually an effortless falling into things as they have always been. To become responsible for peace makes clear the fragile and the solid, the truth and the falsehood, the life and the death of absolute responsibility.

The art of thinking cancels thoughts of war. Thought, as laid out below, only leads to peace. The issue remaining, then, assumes to make up for the wars of the past. In particular WWI and WWII have an enormous debt in the form of lost lives, souls, sins, evil, cancer from the bomb, and many, many others. Although the author was not alive at that time, he knows that only evil has come from war in the world; no good at all. People usually think that the absence of a war against some power averts a greater evil. Still, destiny remains the same.

By destiny, peace stops war. The responsibility is ours to make the list of responsible activities and to answer by life that irresponsible activities are the knowledge of good and evil. So we make our list, as though we are going shopping, and we order ourselves to act responsibly in the name of the Father, the Son, and the Holy Ghost. Deviance from responsibility is sin. The further he applies himself to responsibility, the greater the holiness in his life.

The art of responsibility includes all things in the world, each as well, and the burden is shifted whenever necessary. People who form a group, design his or her own style for this. Ignorance, then, does not admit to shared responsibility, and this was Christ's burden; He was responsible for the people of His time, and now in our own small way in the here and now, we can share our responsibility with the rest of the world.

If we do not accept responsibility for everything in the world, then we do not pass back into the garden. There are other gardens, minors of the garden of good and evil, such as duality non-duality, power and non-power, love and hate . . . I point this out metaphorically, as they are branches of the tree of life, echoes of good and evil. The responsibility to power identifies the parallel of the metaphor. That which is paired with other, even non-dualistically in the mind, is in the Garden of Good and Evil. Duality means that nature attaches fixation on two objects of people. So under good and evil is duality non-duality, love hate, and so on. The resolution of these pairs in the mind toward the absolute non-duality resolves back into God. The person and the object, for instance potentially resolve into one, principal or absence.

The seeds of doubt in the mind are deep indeed. One could doubt Christ's power, the way, compassion, or another quality. Doubt and truth by trust realize to cause responsibility known. Pairs of causes for responsibility of a mental order are more powerful than the actualization. This means, in short, that mental protection is equal to spiritual protection. Christ's name is a form of mental protection.

Peace is greater than war. And why? Peace is the starting place of peace. Peace is peace, peace has peace, and peace goes into further peace. Mentioning Christ's name brings the nature of thinking peace. Once one's nature has changed, he tries the art of thinking.

If we try to choose war over peace, we will be turned back and left with sin. It is worse to vote mentally for a war than to spend one's virginity. To vote for a war mentally is to commit the sin in person before God's eyes of murder. Actually the absence of voting for peace, in this regard, is to fulfill the will of the devil. Killing, war, murder, and so on are countered by the good of peace.

War and peace do not need to be together as they are not the same. One may say there is difference in war and difference in peace, so they are the same. Actually the world does not remain the same by sin, but becomes upset again, and Christianity suffers as a whole. We may feel that because the ground remains the same, because the sky remains the same during war, that it justifies war. The reason for this is that we forget that our religion has not explained completely how the mass of people in the world fall prey to the energy of evil, ignorance, doubt, hatred, and fear.

In peace, two known ways explain how to maintain the belief in peace against the screaming horde. The first of these is in psychology. It is called conformity. To conform to war because so many have actually shows the strength of the individual who started wars. He himself must have turned against the world to start the idea of war, the thoughts of war, and the movement in the world called war.

Actually, Christ has the power to revert these actions, and perhaps he has waited all these years merely now to tell us to choose. How do I choose? The answer to this question lies in with responsibility. The positive leads to responsibility, and responsibility leads through life. Responsibility, once it is taken, makes one known, known for standing for a moment in God's eye in infinity and eternity, and accepting that he himself is first in the mind with responsibility. Love comes into the matter as a prime motive for going to heaven. The right path reflects the trust that responsibility brings. For instance, if I were to feel someone felt no love, then my business is to find a way for that someone to love again. Again, if I felt someone had no responsibility, it is my business to see to it that he finds the truth of responsibility in Christ, the Father, and the Holy Ghost. The author has not gained the responsibility of God but, rather, has taken the responsibility to add to responsibility. My point here is that one can increase responsibility in the soul, the mind, and the body infinitely, and the reader may find that the door has been left just ajar for responsibility to enter.

Food and Responsibility

We use food with responsibility. Without this, one hardly deserves food. People are starving, so we do not throw out food. It is not a joke that eating is a true art of responsibility. The art of responsibility then, induces us to eat for peace. The prayer at the table is spoken over the food that the continuance of our lives by eating will be known only for bringing peace to the world.

Christ himself broke bread for many reasons. One of these was for peace. Another was for holiness. He asserted that one takes the good toward the responsibility. Therefore, the Holy Communion of His soul, or body, means that we are eating responsibility.

Food is a gift to us from God. Fulfilling His will in the world may include eating to reduce anger or to please Him. Love comes when we have eaten, not when we are hungry. Hungry people act differently, and it is a responsibility to eat for peace and to eat for charity. Love only happens when we are not out of our minds for a meal, and to bring this love and responsibility to others has a high reward.

So a blessing for food is this: "In the name of the Father, the Son, and the Holy Ghost, in the name of Mary, Mother of God, may the food we are about to receive bring responsibility for the world to me, to my wife. May I be able to join Christ and His people to cause peace. May I survive another day to eat again, to gain more knowledge, and to find responsibility again. From the bottom of my heart, may we be able to join the rest of the world in peace. This food is the cause of peace, Christ is the cause of peace, and the Holy Spirit makes it so." The prayer invokes the Holy Trinity and Mary. Of course, it is hardly a drop of the prayers needed for peace and responsibility; it is one prayer of an infinite variety, already available to us in the here and now.

To give food is double positive and rewarding. On the one hand, it brings the gift of life to another, while on the other it brings the benefit of giving the gift of life to another. Actually, giving food to a hungry individual even once gains a seat in heaven.

Money
Economically, irresponsibility has uniformly guided monetary use.

Materialism and
The materialist is one of the most dangerous to responsibility. He or she sees the world in terms of his own gain and could not aid, truly, the employment of love. The practice of love should be continuous. One should not become demanding of the kind of love one likes most. The truth explains to use only a little positive and not to become greedy for the attention of God. Actually, the desire to fulfill one's own aims is not responsible at all. One should avoid gaining one's own desire in this world or in the spirit world to the point that one does not know why.

Material possessions are generally valueless to anyone except for their function. The sin of excess is known. Materialistic desires negate the will of God and Christ and are therefore a sin. The absence of materialism is holy. He who worships objects worships nothing. There is a value to really not believing in object as God contacts Him.

A mind related to objects does not really value the person. Here, materialism means the worship of internal objects. So if I praise my emotion, value it, love it, then I am putting something before the love of God. To believe in oneself firstly believes in Creation. To believe in oneself is not to pray to oneself but, rather, to increase the belief in God. Putting aside internal objects like knowledge, the self, all things known, is to put the holy self of Christ at the highest.

When the known itself drops away, does it mean we feel true love? It means we have gotten out of objects. We know the self or the person is not an object, but how do we get out of ourselves completely? Not only is the person a subtle phenomenon, but he or she can be an "object" of thought internally. To identify completely only with people and the higher selves is to forget oneself. One can fill the absence in oneself with other people, with awareness, with consciousness, and with the Divine in any form.

Often we are not as perfect as we think. We think we have achieved something when actually our own imperfections are neither know to ourselves nor to others. God knows everything, but it is best kept secret that he only reveals certain things to us in our life. The meaning here is that we are blind to our own evils, great or small, do not know them, are unaware of them, and cannot control ourselves. To spend our lives in some particular practice, such as discovering a single fault in good in evil, shows responsibility. This is particularly true with eternity. It is nearly impossible to eternally cure something, as we have seen from some of the great errors of the past.

Materialism relates to absence. The complete absence of all things fills the self with the perfection of the divine. The emptiness of phenomena, people, materialism, and the future imply the adaptation and assumption of all points of view to Christ. One who accomplishes this achieves the degree of knowledge of holiness he requires. Further, this too may be void and refilled. It is best to accomplish this with no thought to self.

If we believe in the materialistic, how can we say we believe in love? Love is absence. Absence can be all things, but the absence of materialistic belief implies their fullness of spirit.

Responsibility without materialism requires a perfect form of purity. Responsibility is purity insofar as the mind acquires responsibility in the way of the saints. Christ had the ultimate responsibility for the evil and sin in the world. He Himself took all of our sins of war and healed them. The responsibility of the wars since that time is a very great guilt and a sin against Christ in person.

The responsibility for thoughts, minds, hatred, love, and greed in other people's minds is possible. On this note, we choose peace. The choice of peace known is based on the sin believing in war. To claim, to suggest, to acquire these evils of negativity is to know that choice is possible. I have heard that a technique exists for "choicelessness"; this should not concern us. What others do with religion is the opposite of oppression. To accept them and tolerate them is a perfection leading to peace. The art of Christian negativity is not known; the joy and love we feel in His presence is not meant to close us off from bringing others to some aim. The directions we give each other can also be mental, spiritual, and full of love. The responsibility is not just to change others, the way we change from being hungry to full; it is really about finding our own corner of life for others.

For example, I may learn a great deal about Christ and Christianity for others. This effort is not useless; rather, it is like the lecture I hear when I go to church. The minister tells me about the world and Christ, and after that, I remember to be kind, to go even further with peace every moment, and to help others' minds to feel better.

Becoming responsible and following through to the highest level one can and will bring a very high form of love into one's life. One gets the reward of Christ's love and respect, while at the same time, one's own sense of value naturally increases. Increases in responsibility are possible globally. One must be sure the responsibility is perfect not only in relation to the specific aim, but also in relation to the future. At the very least, we should be sure there is an alternative in the future for people to add or subtract some particular aspect of our blessing unless it becomes a curse.

Subtlety and

Sometimes people become obsessed with subtle phenomena. These should not take priority over responsibility.

Absence and

Absence easily succeeds the mind toward responsibility. With Christ's blessing, one may find one's own way.

The Body, and Soul, and Responsibility

When the body and soul are one, the effort of responsibility gains a stronger foothold in life. Profoundly the mind and body unite in their effort toward some particular aim, such as a job to feed the children, peace, or maintaining a relationship. The body deserves the utmost respect and regard. The body is the place where we live.

Responsibility for the body of oneself seems easier than for another's. Having responsibility of another's body can cannot be taken. I am not just talking about taking care of someone in a hospital. What the author intends here is that we love each other's body with our soul. To take this responsibility means that we are so careful with our own body that we are careful with all people's bodies. The body is a sacred temple of worship, designed by God.

We should not use the body, and we should not abuse the body. Being responsible with the body means many things. One of these is to feed and clothe and bathe the body. Christ's body leads to the Holy Communion. Our body is just as valuable in God's eye as Christ's, although we may not have the same degree of holiness.

How we feed ourselves tells others how much we love ourselves. The sin of gluttony we know means to take too much. To eat just a little, and healthy food, means that we treat the body with the respect deserving of someone made in God's image.

Cleanliness too leads to holiness. We should wash ourselves, thinking of the Divine. Actually, clean or dirty is not the point. Cleanliness here is used in the sense of purity or virginity. A virgin mind of cleanliness can be lost or regained, although of course it is best to remain pure from the beginning.

The Art of Trust

The Art of Betrayal

To betray a known individual or group, the mind fulfills a specialty in self abnegation. It is possible to isolate all causes in a particular way of Christianity; meanwhile, to betray negative or positively in the mind with various quality such as good, evil, truth, falsehood, fire, water, earth, air known now toward peace only.

To go further then, derivatives of said proclamation toward and past peace for eternity decides reality and actuality as perceived in the mind of the archangels. To certify that all knowledge is known for betrayal is known impossible. Similar cases exist for intelligence elementally.

So on the individual level, the art of betrayal is the art of peace. The consequences to suffering of the thought of world war, by an individual are momentous. Greater than all is the angel of peace; yet God walks on the earth to make peace in actuality happen. And why? This is God's wish.

The art of betrayal answers the art of trust. It is forbidden to betray to the extent that a war begins. If betrayal becomes greater than trust, then one must answer to the art of peace. If betrayal becomes greater than the art of peace, then one must answer the art of positive. To really dig into the matter, one considers betraying the known toward peace. The art of known is known.

Betrayal can break the world. Thinking about countered results changes the mind from evil to good. The everlasting truth that betrayal is good and evil does not comply with the evil of war. And why? Betrayal among mortals denies evil briefly without one's own knowledge. The art of functionality forbids the result of betrayal toward war. The reason functionality becomes the known not to betrayal is that functionality is known in all walks of life. Betrayal does not know the sin of murder, nor its induction. The cause of betrayal is known. The name of Christ protects, but evil is powerful too.

When I think of betrayal, I think of actually turning from one side to the other. It is always complex, and there is someone dying. For instance, in peace, one betrays the world to war, it is either positive or negative or known. The known becomes the known, the positive, positive evil, negative, negative evil, and then there is a war. The leader says, "You can have a war." It means that betrayal is an art of peace. Just to betray is enough, but the betrayal becomes peace. So whether people understand, care, or wish to go to hell because of their beliefs, the art of peace is the answer.

Subjectivism and Responsibility

Subjectively, responsibility seems like most other phenomena. So how do we know responsibility and how do we maintain it subjectively. Subjective responsibility springs from the sense of self. This sense is an inner voice of morality, like the conscience. Responsibility aims at decisions to bring the positive to others, to act positively, and to gain knowledge, or experience. Reality and religion combine in this regard to create the truth of responsibility.

The causes of responsibility in our nature are precious subjectivity. To believe and to show responsibility define a life that brings the positive. Faith that God or Christ will help us is useful, while at the same time, to be powered by these is heaven, is to be powered by us and humanity on earth too. So the right motivation in life goes deeper into the mind or soul, thus bringing a wellspring of positives.

Subject moves toward these. The subject ideas, thinking, and routes lead himself to primarily the arts. Responsibility at first decides on one point, such as to fulfill the will of God. Maturity of responsibility endures throughout our life. Responsibly subjective, subjectively responsible matches objectivity for at that level, the result in the world is the same. Compassion, a known starting point for responsibility, maintains subjective responsibility. Actually, if we forget compassion, responsibility will fail.

Evil compassion is bred of ignorance, while negative compassion has painful emotionality. The emotion of pain, subjectively reminds one that the negative is universal. To find the good in the evil is to step into another dimension, such as love. That is to say that when there is some evil within us, for instance in our compassion, then we try love, faith, trust, or other to find a safe place to look for responsibility.

Subjective evil entails a result of responsibility. If we see any evil in the world around us, within us, or in religion, we act immediately, without thinking. Positive subjectivity and negative subjectivity can can't cannot make a world of evil, for the individual or other. This is because subject is only self subject, whereas an evil objectivity infects everything. That is why war is not peace in both worlds, whereas the subjective individual and the objective one do not believe in responsibility in the same way.

In this sense, then subjectivity wins on the individual level and fails on the mass level. However, historically during the phase of objectivity, the wars have been on a larger scale and involved more cruel and unusual techniques for making people suffer.

For peace, the case for subjectivity is stronger. From the objective standpoint peace is possible; from the subjective standpoint people are likely to be more different. So objectively, facts speak, while subjectively, the person speaks. In this way, objectivity takes less responsibility for others because it is less compassionate while a duality of subjectivism and objectivism in a single individual is possible. In that case, subjectivism is the individual, while objectivism is the world.

So the individual in Christianity is subjective. Material is objective. The reason for this is that objectivity is a universal science, while subjectivity is individual. Individuality is a powerful key to universal responsibility.

Book VIII

The Christian Art of Thinking

Christ does not like flaws in His thinking. Thinking in general is an art worthy of a huge amount of effort. Thought tends to be the way of this time period, yet no counterproductive thought should be allowed by the society of Christians. Toward a world wide way of thinking, one would like to specify the possibilities available.

One of these is the thought specific way known so very well to us. This consists of thinking a particular thought and then analyzing objectively what that thought's quality is. For example, some thinking objectively is not thinking subjectively or so both parties think. The actuality of God thinking mind has one quality of infinity. This quality may also be eternal but depends on the art of thought. The reason for the art of thought is that we need the right intention behind our thinking to guide. One might try to think of a thought guide for all of us or say that known is thinking.

We may think today, in the here and now, in our soul. Our soul acts in various ways, and these may focus on a part of the mind, such as thinking. So that there is no confusion, one would like the capacity of thought to be the capacity of the soul.

Within this capacity for thinking, believe God knows thoughts, but also that Christ is His compassion. Similarly if the qualities we like are such and such, then the thinking directs these in the soul or mind. In a stage after mind, one thinks in that stage, of the thoughts of the person. For the explorer type, of god, the intention is to know the thoughts of God, or to express so. In other words, thinking of the unlimited may open a doorway to purity or goodness.

Beyond the capacity of thinking are other aspects of mind; one of these, for example is clarity. It is important to keep thinking clear. Hazy fuzzy thinking might cause accidents. This aptly true if, for example, we think less and less clearly while drinking alcohol and run off the road. Another aspect of mind shows emotion. Emotional thinking controls the states of mind that run us into war.

For the art of thinking, one might consider any quality of thinking. In this sense, one learns to think to avoid the negative; a master might think to avoid evil, even for the whole society. A child can think, a gifted child thinks of compassion. Christ was gifted in the thinking of God. There are other arts.

Almost any art of thinking passes into the capacity of the thinking mind. These include functionalism, an important point in a dangerous world, specific, general, associative, memorial, and many others, for instance 99 percent associative and 0.25% emotional, 0.25 percent rational, 0.25 percent directional, and 0.25 percent spacing out. A full degree of thinking includes the capacity for intelligence, for as we all know, the intermeshing levels are called mind, or thinking mind.

Further, thought includes all the capacities of mind but one—capacity itself. I will leave this for later. So within the mortal mind, there may be 100% capacity for thought. Within 100 percent there is an infinite variety of combinations, and that alone by number.

In the following pages, I will take several aspect of thinking that should give the reader enough example to figure many others. The key to these pages is to be aware of thought as though it is the soul itself. Moreover, whereas the soul is thought, purity is thought, the guide is thought, the nature of mind is thought. This means that in the many aspects of the divine soul is the singular awareness of God, Christ, or a particular angel.

So for the infinite creations of God is also the infinite aspects of thinking. So within infinite is the simple. In similarity, the singular, in difference the same, in philosophy the truth. Therefore without objects one's soul is in purity. It may take great faith to figure out how this is so. For instance, God's great mind may exist in many ways as many small ways toward a singular aspect of thought. So other arts of Christianity can apply to thinking.

Speculation aside, a guide to life is there too; the guide is a friend of God. A friend to all people, Sufi, Ju, Hindu, Taoist, Buddhist, Christian, subjectivist, naturalist, and so on. The guide may know the protector and think well of him or her. Each of us has a guardian angel and that is why that is known. So our thinking does not necessarily flow from ourselves, from God in particular, or from our upbringing.

Another art of thinking is an art of inspiration. Thinking may be inspiration, inspiring, inspirational, or it may be one of other many qualities. Dividing thinking into these categories or qualities is useful for a number or reasons. Also uniting thinking under a single ethic of peace, by marriage, for instance is also highly positive. It is generally not necessary to think of objects by the art of subjectivism. It, meaning any object in particular, is non object thought of the person, saint, priest, friend, angel . . . So many arts exist for thinking.

The first to learn is the art of functional thinking for peace. Primarily, one specifies history in actuality by the race, the world unites in reality toward peace against nuclear wars. The human race, as we know, is diverse. Peace is differse, so this is one point in common. It is a sin not to think of actual peace, and it is a sin to think of something other than actual peace. Thought has always been there, and actual peace too. The actual guide of peace is Christ in person, while the thought guide is a minor angel. When we are children, we don't play with fire because it burns. In this sense, our parents look out for us on high.

Function thinking, then, begins where we are. In the here and the now, we will not cause an accident for ourselves; because of this, we will not cause them for others being self mindful. So what we do to ourselves is the here and now of what we do unto others, even in our dreams, our visions, and our nightmares. Love is the way in the here and now, and we may learn to functionally protect someone. This may consist of mentally controlling our thoughts, or learning to know ourselves by thought perfectly, in the sense that we can reduce rape. This is the first moment of the here and now. The second moment then has thinking for checking our result. Then as the third stage sets in, we take care of ourselves, too.

In the event that new stages develop, the fourth might be to pray for something for others. The next might be the contemplative stage, as we go through the rest of our day, like today, considering all things of religion until the next five stages arrive. At that point, the secondary stage begins with a new series of arts of Christianity. After a few weeks or years, the practices moves on. We begin anew and try new things. The arts in this book are really quite temporal.

Another practice in the here and now of thinking is of the body. One stage of this is to let our thinking join our soul in the body. Physically, one might begin by walking. Learning to walk in prayer for instance for peace, is very useful at this time. The next practice on a walk might be to release the soul's peace in the world outwards. This kind of transmission is like a prayer, or like a soul in a car. Alternatively, when we get into a car, we have to be more careful. So in our caution, it will never be enough absolutely. Eternally, infinitely, and perfectly will still not be enough absolutely.

In a very peaceful environment, such as a monastery, different soul experiences begin to happen. Things happen everywhere, but chaos usually takes the upper hand. It is worthwhile to unconfound this. So in the monastery of a particular place, a group may pray for a specific period for one thing to work out in the world well. That is to say, they might begin at the beginning and go to the present point by point against wars of evil. These monks might also say actual prayers over the sin of murder to alleviate it, a little at a time. It takes a great deal of effort, time, and patience to break these habits in others. So at that time, one will go to the length of peace to stop a war, violence, a disease, or some other negative phenomenon. For instance, as the world wishes for peace, even one monk can save the world.

When we can maintain functionalism in the here and now, we move on again. This stage becomes one of mastering the arts of life, such as farming, walking, fishing, talking, and so on. So the second art of thinking is talking. The art of speech may make known an attitude of positivism. It is shared equally among the race.

A long example is necessary. A man and a woman live together on a farm. It is time to plant. The man says, "Go and fetch me the shovel." The woman replies, "Fetch it yourself." One can see at a glance that the negative effect of these words on one another serves to increase the negative and to deny the positive. The correct phrasing begins with the positive and ends with the positive. Any form of emotional negativity is meant to be excluded from God's world simply because we can. It is a mortal test, to see who fulfills the positive good ways of the known versus the negative good ways of the known. This leaves the mortal to choose the positive or the negative. Between good and evil and positive and negative is the known, while positive good, negative good, and positive evil and negative evil are all possible to mentally defeat but one per human round. So during the period of knowing another or several others, the art of Christian thinking is the art of the positive.

Various arts of thinking apply; one is the art of intelligence. Another is the art of associating. The art of finding your own way too makes the meaning of the art of Christianity your own. By intelligence for instance, the art of good and evil means that we are thinking of Christ in a slightly different way. So for thinking, we think of Christ or the one of our choosing; for intelligence the one of our choosing, and so on. This leads directly to infinity for any combination inclusive of human nature, mind, or other has the door to infinity.

The art of thinking further elaborates into speech. One way for this to happen is as described by specifying exactly what our soul is thinking to everyone. Further, one may then become generalized. The generalized form of the art of thinking applied to speech goes through the full run of thinking in the course of a life for the aims of the positives. Christ then did not perfect our speech, but he may in the future by prayer. The next aim of speech becomes to fulfill his nature, or true will.

Speech then becomes an art of making the other feel his love, as noted above. To know him, to love, and to exist in nature is the perfection of language in regard to Christ. Relationally perfecting language in others is an equal endeavor. One method might be to peacefully induce the love of Christ. Another way is to find our own way with language. Further still, one can express this perfection of words with silence.

Silence is an art of speech as well. To maintain the thoughts of love in silence while another does not know our thought only masters after the perfection of trust. Silence is perfect for contemplation, love, and other qualities. It is important not to fail this point. It is the silence of thought that brings the method of language to a tee. Actually, and phase of thought itself can be a perfection for speech. To fulfill this all the way to Christ and above is the ultimate. One might calmly talk a woman out of a bad habit to break the silence of oppression.

Speech gains the power to control a little too. Control may only be employed in this regard for positives. That is to say that if harm, sin, or negativity come from one's speech one takes only one's own responsibility for it, and begins to pray from there. Speech gains power of thought by thought too. Furthermore, speech gains care infinitely by perfection of positive. Listing the arts of God as the arts of positive is forbidden fruit.

It is not possible to replace Christ, especially on the cross. His speech, however maddening, could not have been spoken by a mortally sane man. Perfection of this nature submits to the ultimate willingness to love and be loved. This is how his speech has worked toward the positive.

A part of life is the permanent wholeness of the world of Christ. To truly understand all things is only possible by Himself. Gaining an idea that one has understood is linguistically possible but unthinkable. To leave in our thinking without coming back to the truths of peace is ethically untenable. Arguing the facts of his life is not the intention of the man of God. Christ is the holy and the art of speech plays the art of thinking. Thinking here and now precedes the art of speech while they overlap. Thought precedes mind, while mind absorbs thought and speech. Toward the perfection of speech is not only infinite but also singular fragment heavenly. To sing or to pray in ordinary words was once a lost art; rather than to return, the art here is to proceed into the future life a perfect form of peace warrior. To make peace of functionalist language in prayer is one art, but there are other arts that lead to that same goal. Actually, the absolute wishes for this with his mind in our thoughts. Hatred, greed, aversion, and pain are the answer to not making peace our only capacity. God may be dead, but His people live on praying for them to join him again. This marriage of peace symbolizes is a perfection of known combination. It is forbidden to marry for other opposite of peace.

The arts of speech include the art of letters, words, phrases, grammars, languages, and so on. But there are many when there is unity in His name. Christians, however, do not foresee all problems with other religions. The blind lead the blind, thusly go we toward language. Thought, therefore, awaits truths of peace; the fulfillment is an earthly global movement already well enough along the way. Going further still, the combination of functionalism and trust as an art of thought makes the nature of the Word known. That which is true is peace. That which is false is less peace. To meet in the human limitation of all language, knowns, arts, and trusts may solve a few problems, and the greater art of world peace is brought by the greater leader ever known. The peacemaker is the son man, and his brother is the devil. God on high watches to let him die in peace.

Specifics of identifying causes of Christ and Christians makes the reality of another word worth mentioning. Any other word toward peace or positive brings the light to earth of the truth of peace. The art of betrayal is damnable. Evil lurks in all beings for him who betrays the peace, the love, and absolutes of life. A reason for why it is not the same at peace and beyond peace gives the mind peace internally. We die individually if we are not in the way of peace, and return to be baptized in the art of peace.

The subtle forms of peace, then, begin to expand in our mind until the first marks appear in the world of the art of peace. The art may be many things, but cannot be any art that has a mark of violence or not peace. Assuming it is possible in a few years deserves note. One must actually attain it now in the church and deal with the consequences. They must be positive. All movements have brought us to peace and it has been under the thumb of Christ that the last wars were fought. My belief is that he did not mean to do so, but rather that he himself could not control the evil in the world. It's tough luck to have to go back to no money on Christ so to speak, but positives almost always come along to earn the right back is the way of Christ as well.

The art of thinking past problems toward peace is one category. To elucidate, the various capacity of the person play in each way and into the new specifically. These forces are known, while there are unknown ones as well. Good and evil is not really the point of the peace. Each phenomena in the world and each thought and deed singularly and in all knwons is more to the point. So these are complex or simple; to use thought is a simple and direct method to addressing the issues confronting the world. And why? For that very reason that one unified peace is possible by thinking. And why again? For that thinking is common to each in his own way.

What is on the other side of problems as we aim to peace? One of these factors is known; it is a racial unification of the world in peace. Various factors are known; one of these is the art of the positive, another is the art of responsibility. These arts are not known to all of us, but by thought it is possible to communicate rightly, to join the world again for an absolute decision. This is possible in the here and now, while thinking maintains losses to evil. People tend by thinking to think of the nature of thought. This nature is the actual peace nature of Christ. That is all He really wanted. The absolute words of Himself are not completely interpreted. Many of his people died to memory. The thinking our nature is not the only way; the truths of Christ fulfill thinking, whereas, other factors are required such as functionality, desire, emotion, and so on.

In brief the author will describe a few levels of thinking. The first in the adult stage is the acknowledgement of oneself. At that first moment, when the door opens as they say, the person realizes others think as well. That is a perfect moment to say peace. The confusion or clarity at that time may bring the mind to a state of manipulation.

The next stage is one in which the manipulation attain a new factor. This may be many things but might consist of intelligence. The thinking becomes deeper and may even apply to knowledge. All along these stages, there is a sin for all of us. That sign is that we are there in the self, under the heavens, successfully remaining alive. Christ is with us, in the form of the loving peace keeper. His brothers and sisters remain alive with him as well. Life towards the wise may bring peace into the heart.

The thinking then settles down into the absolute level of a contemplation of peace or another positive angel. These kinds of activities do not apply toward evil, but the purpose is not non-evil in the form of good, but rather the art of good for others. By the art of prayer, the maintenance of thought is possible. In this case, the meaning is that prayer and thought join thinking toward peace or the aim.

Over time the second thought of generations begins. It is more difficult to unite all thought in the world than it is to make peace. And why—because one thought of a ninety year old and the thought of a boy are quite different. On the other hand, man and woman in the garden may not even no themselves differently. It seems known that people do not know their predecessor's thoughts, while many individuals' thought seem the same in clarity not content. The clarity toward actual peace thinking comes from the connection of the body and mind. Remember there are two arts to body and mind, the physicalis and the monkal. So new arts develop of peace in relation to mind and body, maybe even new gymnastic!

The generation before remembers the one before that, maybe even associatively. The prayers tell us that all we are is all we were. So our present thought is actually a combination of all things that have transpired in the world. The effects of these events however, vary widely; if we live in one part of the world, we "knew" more people who had seen war, or in another people who only spoke of peace. Christ in this case, is the Creator. So we are born live and die in a world of peace; it has begun, been done, and continued by the already known.

One should rest in the peace of the world and bring it by love to the rest of the world; from there one rests in the thinking with the gifts of actual peace from the angles, Christ and God. Thinking not qualifies thinking as a complete rest of the soul. The soul can rest in the body and the mind can think. The soul always stays with the body, while thinking can be mental or physical. One's body has the soul, so the body's soul can think all the while, greater even than the brain.

Ordinarily most of us feel that our thoughts work out the way they are thought. Literally speaking thinking is thought. So in actually, something must happen for us to think, while at the same time new formulations from God come toward us. Our thinking meets these prayers, thoughts, dreams, as well as the here and now. To have a thought is also to think newly of something in one's mind in the following thought. Therefore thinking of may also think to; thinking to may think where; thinking where may think how, and so on. Key, or main, thinking chains are not the purpose of advancing thinking. One's thinking can cannot improve, while can't cannot cause evil. One's thinking can also improve the points known of impurity, disease, accidents, ignorance, personality, hatred, and so on, all the way through to the fact that improving no longer seems the important but rather the love of actual peace, the love of Christ, the path of Good, truth, and justice.

Perfection of thinking does not involve some particular thought of God. Even an infinite future in heaven does match the perfection of thinking. This means that thought is more a relative art of our lives here and now for survival now against the forces that surround us. Thoughts seem to change, while the prayer results seem to remain the same. In an infinite future, with infinite peace and infinite positive ahead of us, nothing seems to change here and now. The unchanging here and now may turn the here and now into a prayer for peace. This means that the things around us name our prayers.

To open the mind in the here and now is to open the soul. An open mind is one that is receptive to all thoughts and prayers. To receive is to give and to give again. Actually receptivity means to be passive. We may rest our minds in peace inducing thoughts day in day out, year after year, but it is more important to take action. Action after careful thought may not produce a result; it is more important to think then act, then return to the thinking. Analytical thinking produces very positive results. Analytic thinking is practical, but is still only thought. So we think, then we act. To analyze means to study a problem from various points of view.

Analytic thinking too, has a guide. Thinking we can answer a prayer, in the name of Christ is one result of analysis. The results of analytical thinking are always peace positive. One can specialize in some particular content, such as good and evil, or one can think freely of anything, peace. So in this case, all thoughts lead to peace.

Thinking can also be resting in responsibility. If all thought is responsible, all things go according to the perfect choice. When thought, choice, prayer and other factors all lead to peace, peace is there, peace is known, and peace is actualized.

Thinking also aims the person toward the higher aims of morality. Immorality is always negative, while morality is always positive. It's as simple as that. With wisdom, good and evil fall to morality, responsibility, trust, love, and the will of God. His anger subsides.

Thinking may show attachment or non-attachment. After many years of practice, such as the art of loving Christ, attachment and non-attachment themselves may fall away to a perfection of resting in this love. Individuals may think their way on many branches of the human tree. No one except God can do all of the thinking, and it may be known that God takes time, relative to human nature to proceed with human thought. On earth, our thinking is quite limited. Alternatively after some time, one's thinking may increase in efficiency to counter sexual problems, impurity, desire, greed, aversion, hatred, ignorance, and on and on.

Thinking may be divided or undivided. To focus on the known as God or Christ is also to focus on eternity or infinity. God can stop time altogether; thinking during the stopping of time can become expansive. Ten years' worth of thought may occur when time stops, but it has to come from somewhere. The guide of life informs the person thinking of thinking. Prayer time may stop toward positive or specifically toward peace, yet good and evil in time break back into time when they lean toward a known functional evil such as war, rape, crime, and such.

Divided thinking is really thinking set upon more than one topic such as good and evil. Divided thinking is primarily dualistic. Undivided thinking primarily rests upon one perfection such as Christ. I am what my thoughts tell me, what Christ tells me, and what God tells me. He who only focuses on Christ focuses on the Son of God. Resting in wisdom of the good leads to the art of thinking.

The cause of faithful thinking is known. Other forms of known thinking by cause realize singularity in this regard or multipolarity. With all known forms of Good and Evil thinking in the body, the question then becomes how do we make peace by thought? One answer is with mental control. Another is with giving, a form of though itself. Another is with trust, another is to turn the other cheek. Another is by philosophy. The form of sharing with others our thoughts enforces the peace, because all thinking causes peace. Otherwise, there is no thinking at all. This is actually a conservative point of view.

The same thinking by nature is thinking in the known. The known, again, shows existence as a quality of being. So thinking known is most of our thoughts. The soul is a part of the known as well. The art of thinking, then, shows known thought. To think opens the doors to the soul and the holy and the holy and the soul make the art of thinking an Art.

The art of thinking includes each and every capacity of the mind. All of these become a part of thinking and objects of our thinking. Thinking of the positive rains the great ideas of Christianity into the soul. All of these are positive.

The Art of Peace

Mind is capable of so much; the various factors we know have been known and taken for granted. The factors of ignorance are so common that they are not even known as the only ones. They are actually many. In the diversity of the many, become a complex way of fragments of the introspection for autobiographical memory. These memories of culture not only bring peace by nature, but nature causes memory. The world's simplicity is natural; peace causes life and life's causes are peaceful known afore life supported humanity. Bones, blood, the organs, the brain, the nervous system, bring life to us, rather than make life known. For instance, the brain does not let us die even if we try. Christianity supports only peace in the world, by the cross, Jesus, the Christians the angels and God Himself. His eye sees peace in the world before Creation.

Peace known is known peace. Difference known is known difference. Your own known is your own known. Actuality known is known actuality. Knower known peace is peace known knower. Difference known peace is known actuality peace known your own peace difference. It seems difficult to understand, while the author is known as well in this regard.

Therefore peace becomes the known at all times by all causes, so that Christ's cause of peace remains the same known. Angels become peace toward the aims of the Lord. The Lord is the maker of the cause's nature, while nature known cause of nature becomes capacity known. This logic known by cause becomes infinite by practice. Doctrine awakens Christ the known at female male virginity causes known. Christ's nature of nature itself causes Himself the improvement. World improvement depends on world agreement by each Christian who can not say peace.

There arts cause known known. Good arts cause known known good and evil. Arts of good and evil simplify to defeats of beast known. Simple causes good. Not only causes known. Difference known cause of peace, same known cause of peace. The known itself is a cause of peace. And why? The known is known for life, and life is peace.

Here and now known peace known can't cannot can peace.

The various arts of thinking are the arts of peace. One may rest the soul in the associations, the feeling, the individual himself, and so on. These are all arts of peace. Resting is not the only possibility. Activity based on these functions takes up the art of peace as well. We might find our mind 100 percent resting; the intelligence rests in the resting of associations, actually every factor in ourselves known might rest; at that time, the known equals peace.

Peace is not our only thinking, however. We might rest our thinking as we contemplate God. Actually if we are lucky we will get food every day as well as rest our thinking in God's thinking. The human race generally has something in common with everyone, so we can think in that as well. It is also possible to think of thinking.

The here and now is known for difficulty but it is the best place for the art of Christian mystery. Each of our thoughts is a mystery. We may wonder how the thought appeared there, but more important questions are practical in relation to the negative. God is great, and God is good, but at the same time, when we feel Christ's love, we could be thinking of fulfilling something positive or useful in the world to please him.

Even when God is angry, he wants peace. It has always been my belief that God does not get angry, that the Bible was wrong about that. How could someone so smart try something as small and negative as anger? Not only this, but perhaps He expresses anger because that is what the human race is feeling. I think it makes sense that God expresses everything he creates. That explains how God can be everywhere.

When there is peace everywhere, within and without, God remains the same. He never changes. So His wrath is really not a war. After He decides not to have anymore war, we know this because we feel like stopping the war ourselves. When God wants something we want something. So actually the peace movement is a movement of God. The war movement has been seen before, and the tired old man Christ tries to tell us this but we don't listen. So in the long run, the solutions to peace are a mystery, a revelation, or a dream; to fulfill brings a world surprise. We have to try it ourselves and turn the other cheek to the peace movement knowing God wishes to see peace in the four corners of the world.

The perfection of the art of peace identifies how peace flows on in the world from Christ to us. We can not send the art of peace into the world in our soul and our mind. In fact, all of our lives do go to the art of peace. Simplicity is the mind and love is the soul. Peace flows from simple love for all people, although faith in the world for peace is equal in this regard. The known of the positives Christianity make peace with or without our knowledge and memory is the body, the blood, and the soul of Christ.

The Art of Morality

What is morality?
    Compassion
    Love
    Positive
    Determining Morality
Morality and the Meaning of Life
    Desire
    Hatred
    Positive
    Status of Morality
Morality and Christ
    Christ's Will
    Humanity and Christ
    Christ's difference

Morality and God
    Angry God

Choice and Morality
    Error
    Truth
    Wisdom
    Right Morality

Morality and Other Religions
  Tolerance
  Trust
  Difference of Ideology

Morality and War
  Compassion
  Right Choice

Morality and Peace
  Right Choice
  Right View
  Right Paradise

Morality and Sin

Morality and Mass Movements
  Same and Difference

Morality and the Church
  The Advisor
  The prayer
  Children

Morality and Righteousness
  Let the Truth Be Known

Evil and Morality
  Wrong Choice

Good and Morality

Feminsim, Racism

The Art of Christian Knowledge

The Knower

The knower is ordinarily called the self, or the person. The knower may also be called the one who knows experience. The knower is the id. The knower may be known or unknown. These are various ways in which the knower's known has subjunctives of the known itself: objects perception, belief in other minds, desire, having in self or other, and so on . . .

The attributes of the knower are either many or one. The knower himself is one, and may call known one or many things by perception. Perception is an attribute of the knower. The knower is the known. The knower knows objects or people. The knower has known. The knower is known.

The knower becomes manifest to herself. The self is known to the knower, is the knower. The knower thus known is made by the elements of creation. The knower knows creation. The knower recognizes the knower. The knower recognizes the known in the knower. The knower feels. The knower might see, hear, feel the body, smell, and taste. The senses are primarily perceptual, while the knower of these is also the perceptual knower.

The knower remains the same. The knower may know difference, too. The knower experiences positive and negative. The knower has the knowledge of good and evil yet does not know the known. Knowledge of the knower by the said knower is knowledge of the known.

The knower self knows other phenomena. The known is in the knower and the knower is in the known. The knower in the known is the knowing. The knowing knower experiences, perceives in the knower the known.

From his one perspective, the knower is always there himself/herself. She cannot forget herself, nor remember another. So in this regard she is everywhere. In other words, because the knower is the knower of all within herself, the knower is the one known to herself everywhere. For her knower, that guide to everywhere is within, in the art of religion.

The knower cannot leave the knower lest he enter heaven; therefore, the form of everywhere is the knower. Everywhere then, the knower is the air to survive must be the water, the necessity. Where everywhere knower is a state of knowing. The knowledge of good and evil to be everywhere the Art of Virginity is everywhere as well.

The knower may be subjective or objective. For the major race of humanity, and the various primary styles of subjectivity. Subjectivity itself can be everywhere in the same way.

Specifically, the Nature of the Knower

The nature of the knower is of intimacy with subject. The knower is akin to awareness. The knower is similar to subject but is a part of subject. The knower may be defined as subject without other aspects of the person. The knower however still maintains as the person.

Nature stays known by the knower. The knower acts like a window to nature. The knower is near the center of the self. The nature of the knower replies to other aspects subject with knower knowns. Skill in the knower is the knower himself.

Knower is known than nature within field of knower (nature is known self nature). Knower in field of variance is changeless knower. Known is changeless. Knower is positive nature of knower positive.

To knower phenomena appear. Self mind remains the same. Difference nature of knower not knowable. In change field of knower phenomena subjective known constant with change phenomena. Mystery of knower existence. Mystery there at all. And why? For dream nature of knower.

Knowing

For the person the state of knowledge is considered knowing. It is continuous; a gap in the knowing is only possible during sleep. Knowing continuously explains that knowledge is the known. The known is continuous, though we may not be aware of it as such. Knowing is like someone passing through a building. The building is the knower, and knowing is the passive activity of the person. If the knower is an element, then knowing is the element within the knower. Knowing is like the hands of a clock while the knower the person looking at it.

Knowing subject is doubly same, while maintaining singularity. To split the mind into subjectivity and objectivity by cannot say equals one self four known. As subjectivity is split into difference and object subject minds equation equals two modalities known one inclusive the other two same. According to objectivity and subjectivity, knowing must remain the same because objectively ago knowing did not change. Differences of subjectivity and objectivity and subject and objectively known subject categorized within objectivity element disclose the invisibility of objectivity itself, the subject, as well as that which we call "difference."

Subjectivity too may be everywhere, because subject is knowing only subject known.

Knowing good and evil is not known knowledge thereof. In particular for example, the names are not the same whereas difference is not the same. The same then could be true of other Christian arts, such as soul, love, compassion, and truth. There is an art to it; putting something everywhere in the world using the soul is more risky than using the mind or love. Perhaps the best thing for this is to just go everywhere sometimes, somewhere too.

Knowing is also a state of the soul. The soul knowing neither good nor evil can proceed not to know God himself. Knowledge of difference and same are not known object or subject. Knowing object as subject is a disidentity with perception so that object known is known not subject. It is an evil fate for people that grammar can structure language to employ or know evil at all. We should therefore not phrase grammar known grammar evil. It is the same for meaning, word, letter, knower, knowing, and many others. The epitome of evil language speaks good until evil arises. Satan was behind this language, whereas God speaking aloud through Jesus could never bring evil; it means that our thoughts, words, silence, state of trust, even our faith, known for evil, do not accord with a perfection that reaches to atheism to escape evil. "In the beginning was the word . . ." This really means to mortals to isolate language that starts actions of evil first, then to isolate another level, such as thoughts, and so on. At various levels, one can isolate knowledge of good and evil, and make the return to Eden.

Knowing is active and passive. The active form relates to knowing the self or subject. Knowing myself very well means that knowing has wisdom. By knowing, the mind moves a little from this to that. For instance, knowing myself does not generally mean that in knowing all about myself is known during the instant. Rather, knowing here means that knowing moves about from bit to bit. Knowing also has the active sense of constancy. Being continuous, knowing maintains subject the same. Knowing has various capacities such as knowing different contents of subject as pain, wellness, positive, and negative. There are also various styles of knowing such as virginal, nonaggressive, and so on.

Another active sense of knowing is in its linguistic capacity. Knowing is not exactly a language of mind but, rather, a natural part of the mind that says rather quietly, "knowing." Specifically, generally, and points in between have a different state of themselves. Knowing may be likened to awareness. Knowing is contemplative while awareness has the sense of awakedness.

Actively again, knowing means something. Grammatically, knowing gains meaning by the life force of experience. So knowing means something to us. This meaning does not have to attain to knowledge of factuality or emotion. Knowing therefore is active self-existence.

There are many states of passive knowing as well. The most obvious of these is the unconscious knowing, or the knowing we have when we are not actively using that aspect. Knowing in this regard is passive in that that knowing is as rest.

Another way in which knowing is passive rests in the receptive aspect. The knower knowing himself need not try to apply this. This is the aspect in which the knower is not other than that very self identity. So in this relation, he himself is receptive to the formation we call knowing. He himself is at once the giver and the recipient of knowing. So there is nothing in knowing unlike knowing.

The nature of knowing is similar. The nature of knowing, descriptively written, is of passive subject. He or she as a person with the capacity for knowledge could not realize a nature other than knowing. That is the true nature of knowing. Subject has the basis of knowing. Experience too, need not apply here, for knowing happens whether or not we have the experience.

Objects such as names, and thoughts proceed into knowing. They are like the knowers knowns. Possession of them, however, is not real. These are like a dream. For Christ, however, the power of the appearance is the source of love. He is also known as the Creator of Knowing, the Knower, and Knowledge.

The art of knowing the body shows the utmost simplicity. Simply put, mind knows who he is. Knowing the body is at the basic level, feeling. After that, it becomes spiritual. All of the aspects of the universe, God, Jesus, angels, have the capability to reside in the body and to be experienced by knowing the body. So at some level, knowing is in the body, and this is a passive art. For instance, one does not have to try very hard so that knowing the body is there.

The body too is capable of knowing the mind. Once the intelligence or knowing rests firmly in the body with the soul, the body gains knowledge, knowing, and known too. So the body reacts to the mind, and the mind reacts to the body. The connection between these two is in the nervous system. As is known elsewhere, the Spirit of God can move anywhere.

The art of knowing the mind too truly attempts ease. The philosophy is somewhat more difficult. This way, the state of knowing becomes involved in the complex array of capacity of mind. For instance, the associative mind can be encountered by associative knowing, mnemonic knowing, and so on. The level of simplicity of pure knowing regains as soul-body knowledge realizes stability in itself.

There are many Arts of Knowing, as is known. Others of these include the art of knowing peace, the art of knowing by specific qualities, and the art of knowing the soul.

Knowledge

Knowledge is of people and objects. Knowledge may also be a knowing sense of having, not having this or that, and others. The knower is usually the one knowing knowledge. So knowledge does not have to conform to be "of" something; knowledge may be "to" someone, "for" someone, etc . . . Subjective knowledge is possible too.

Knowledge is also of life. Knowledge is connected to all forms of internal experience and via the nervous system all external phenomena. It is awareness, consciousness, desire, and itself makes these possible. Knowledge is the capacity to solidify the known.

Knowledge of knowledge is not really good and evil. Knowledge is actually unbiased by nature; knowledge is knowledge, not positive or negative. Only contents of our beliefs can make us say it is or isn't so. So whether we believe particular bits of knowledge are good or bad, right or wrong, scientific or subjective, the truth remains that knowledge itself is constant.

It is interesting that knowledge is the capacity of humans for known. Without knowledge, other functions take over such as language, intuition, and belief. Knowledge is, therefore, currently our primary key to understanding the world and its people. Knowledge is like a very large cup; it can keep filling up but, after a while, begins to turn into wisdom

Knowledge has spirituality as well. The subjectivist forms of knowledge entail the same reality as the objectivist's. Subjectively knowledge makes knowing possible. Subjective knowledge known is the subject. Subject known reflects subject in subject known. The subjectivist who finds her own way in Christianity finds illumination of Christ's love, understanding, and compassion within herself.

Spirituality of knowledge can be the knowledge of creation, Christ, God, or any factor of Christianity. God or the Spirit can surround our knowledge. Knowledge can become saturated with a quality such as wisdom.

    State of mind
    State of soul
Knowledge of Objects
Knowledge of People
Knowledge of Angels
Knowledge of Christ
Knowledge of God

Nature is somehow an entity like a knower. Nature subject (two entities).